ON
HAUNTED
GROUND

Photography by Meagan Rogers

About the Author

Lisa Rogers has lived in a haunted house for twenty-eight years. She attends paranormal seminars and pokes around old buildings in hopes of increasing her understanding of the unseen. Her young adult paranormal novel *Angelina's Secret* will be released in spring 2012. Visit her online at http://talkingaboutghost.blogspot.com and http://author lisarogers.weebly.com.

To Write to the Author

If you wish to contact the author or would like more information about this book, please write to the author in care of Llewellyn Worldwide, and we will forward your request. Both the author and publisher appreciate hearing from you and learning of your enjoyment of this book and how it has helped you. Llewellyn Worldwide cannot guarantee that every letter written to the author can be answered, but all will be forwarded. Please write to:

Lisa Rogers
℅ Llewellyn Worldwide
2143 Wooddale Drive
Woodbury, MN 55125-2989

Please enclose a self-addressed stamped envelope for reply, or $1.00 to cover costs. If outside the USA, enclose an international postal reply coupon.

LISA ROGERS

ON HAUNTED GROUND

THE GREEN GHOST AND OTHER SPIRITS OF CEMETERY ROAD

Llewellyn Publications
Woodbury, Minnesota

FIRST EDITION
First Printing, 2012

Book design by Bob Gaul
Cover art: Ghost © iStockphoto.com/Famke Backx
        Tree © iStockphoto.com/123render
Cover design by Kevin R. Brown
Editing by Patti Frazee

Llewellyn Publications is a registered trademark of Llewellyn Worldwide Ltd.

Library of Congress Cataloging-in-Publication Data
Rogers, Lisa, 1965–
  On haunted ground: the green ghost and other spirits of Cemetery Road/
  Lisa Rogers.—1st ed.
     p. cm.
  ISBN 978-0-7387-3236-7
1. Ghosts—United States. 2. Haunted houses—United States.
3. Haunted places—United States. I. Title.
  BF1472.U6R656 2012
  133.1'2973—dc23
                    2012000735

Llewellyn Publications does not participate in, endorse, or have any authority
or responsibility concerning private business transactions between our authors
and the public.
  All mail addressed to the author is forwarded, but the publisher cannot, unless
specifically instructed by the author, give out an address or phone number.
  Any Internet references contained in this work are current at publication time,
but the publisher cannot guarantee that a specific location will continue to be
maintained. Please refer to the publisher's website for links to authors' websites
and other sources.

Llewellyn Publications
A Division of Llewellyn Worldwide Ltd.
2143 Wooddale Drive
Woodbury, MN 55125-2989
www.llewellyn.com

Printed in the United States of America

Contents

Introduction:
A Letter to the Reader

We all know what they say about those who assume. Now, with that out of the way, I'm still going to assume that either you believe in ghosts or you're at least open to the idea they may exist. It isn't my intention to try to prove their existence, but to relay to you true stories of ghostly encounters my family and I have experienced.

It's probably best to start by saying that we live in a haunted house. I understand the mere words "haunted house" conjure up images of an old, run-down two-story, with most, if not all, of the windows missing or broken and the window shutters precariously dangling out and slamming into the side of the house. Typically, there are bats flying all around, and let's not forget the ever-present full moon.

That isn't the case with our house. Our home is a one-story, with all, thank goodness, of the windows intact, no bats, and only an occasional full moon. In case you need the proper ambience to hear a good ghost story, I'll share with you that, at one time, we did have a black cat; of course, my dogs ran it off, but we did indeed have one.

As my husband Wes would say, these stories aren't "Hollywooded up." You won't be reading about headless horsemen riding through fog-filled valleys terrorizing the innocent. Instead, through our eyes, you'll experience what it's like to see a full-bodied apparition standing in your dining room, to hear your name called when you're alone, and to know that someone you can't see is tucking your young daughter into bed at night.

We bought this house with its first unseen occupant right before we were married in 1984. Over the years, many other entities have come and gone, with some staying for a very long time.

We've raised two wonderful children at this house. Our children are two years apart in age; our daughter Keshia is now twenty-five, and our son Troy is twenty-three. My daughter and I always believed in ghosts while my husband and son did not. At one time, Wes was a self-proclaimed skeptic denying all things pertaining to the paranormal. He not only disbelieved in ghosts, but also thought those of us who did believe were perhaps a little on the unstable side.

Troy is harder to explain. Most of the time, he doesn't like to talk about ghosts or about the strange things he's seen in our home. He states, "I'll admit there's something here. I don't know what it is, but I don't believe in ghosts."

You can probably imagine some fun and sometimes not-so-fun family discussions. For the most part, we try to respect each other's views and opinions on all things, including ghosts, however difficult that sometimes proves to be.

It would be fair to say that Keshia and I share some common traits. Not only do we both believe in ghosts, but we're also both sensitive to their presence. By that, I'm not claiming we have any special abilities. When a ghost is present, we simply know we're not alone.

On occasion, we'll receive impressions about the ghost. We might get a sense of whether the ghost is male or female, an approximate age, what time period the spirit might be from or even an ethnic background. I don't understand myself why, or even how, we're able to do this, which makes it impossible for me to offer an explanation to anyone else. It's just something both of us have always been able to do.

Living with ghosts for twenty-seven years has taught my family and me that there are many things we can't explain—of course, that doesn't keep us from trying. With Wes now also believing in ghosts, together we strive to learn more about those who share with us not only our home, but also our world. We've attended seminars to try to understand what ghosts are and why they're here. We've learned to utilize today's technology by using EMF detectors, digital cameras, and voice recorders, all in hopes of understanding.

Over the years, we have taken quite a journey and I hope you enjoy reading about part of it here. I say part because we are still here, we still have ghosts, and we're still learning.

I: NEW BEGINNINGS

1984

. . . .

In 1984, my fiancé Wes and I began the exciting search for what would become our first home. Unlike other young couples, our needs were very specific and without a doubt a little unusual. We were looking for a house that we could move. Wes's parents gave us ten of the eighty acres he had grown up on for a wedding present.

Our only other requirement for the house was that it needed to be cheap. The size didn't matter and the condition, I was told, didn't matter. Cheap, that would be the selling point. This type of house wouldn't be found through a realtor. No, this type of house would be found by hearing from a friend, who had a friend that had a cousin who had a friend ...

This took some time, but eventually we learned, through the proper channel of friends, about a house in the next town meeting our requirements, so we arranged to go see it. Upon first sight, I could tell it wasn't quite what I'd hoped it would be. The house was small and there were several areas where the siding had fallen off. The brackets that once held the metal awnings in place had rusted through on one side, causing them to droop sideways over the windows, giving the entire house a droopy appearance.

As we walked around the outside of the house, we discovered there was a small room added on to the back that couldn't survive the move. Meaning the house would become even smaller. Trying to look on the bright side, I consoled myself with the thought that the inside might be better.

Well ... it had potential, sort of, if I didn't focus on the gold shag carpet, the bright blue walls, and the peeling wallpaper. Walking into the kitchen, my positive attitude started to wane. The linoleum floor crumbled under our feet, the counters were cracked, and the few existing cabinets had about a hundred coats of paint on them.

I was beginning to wish the house hadn't already met the said requirements, but unfortunately, it had. Trying to maintain our "can do" attitude, we said we'd take it, along with the challenge of fixing it up.

As we walked around the little house discussing the improvements we could make, I felt as though someone was watching us. I believed in ghosts, but I'd never given their existence much thought. I'm not sure why I've always believed, but my theory is a simple one. I think I must've had an encounter with an entity before I was taught not to believe in them.

Whenever I encountered one, I usually got a sense of something about them—and this time was no different. I knew whoever it was wasn't anyone we needed to fear. I felt the entity was a kind, elderly woman who'd probably once lived there. In my mind, ghosts were just a natural part of life and it never occurred to me to mention to Wes the fact that I sensed one in the house. The way I saw it, a ghost was the least of our worries.

We bought the house and started the long process of having it moved to our land. Once the house was in place, we needed to make it livable. The first project consisted of wiring the house for electricity. This project, like all the ones to follow, proved to be more expensive and took much longer than expected.

Racing against the clock to beat our fast-approaching wedding day, Wes got busy outside digging trenches for the water and gas lines while I worked on the inside. The house was in bad shape to start with and moving it had left its mark. Now we had holes in most of the walls, and the floors and ceilings sagged.

In the midst of trying to plan a wedding and all of the work involved getting the house ready for us to move into, I rarely thought about our unseen resident. I knew she was there because even though I was alone in the house, I heard footsteps and I always felt as though someone was watching me.

Ghost or no ghost, we had work to do. Our wedding was right around the corner and our house ... well ... it wasn't even close to being ready. There were still holes in most of the walls and we had no running water and no gas. Since we'd already sent the wedding invitations, we didn't want to postpone the wedding, so we continued with our plans and married on schedule.

After our short honeymoon, we started our new lives together in our rickety little house. We tried to look at it as an adventure. It was, after all, a lot like camping. We had to haul water in from Wes's parents' house and the only cooking we could do was what we could manage with an electric skillet. As it turned out, our new way of living was much more exhausting than adventurous.

On that first night, when bedtime finally rolled around, I was more than ready for some sleep. However, getting married at the end of October and living in a house with no heat wasn't such a good idea after all. It was cold! We jumped into the bed and snuggled down under the covers. As I tried to go to sleep, hoping to at least dream of some place warm, I heard Wes say, "What's that?"

I poked my head out from my cocoon of blankets and saw a green, glowing ball about the size of a grapefruit hovering in the corner of our bedroom.

Shivering, Wes got out of bed to get a closer look. He tried to block the light with his hands. The glowing ball moved around to the front of his hands. Trying to figure out where the light was coming from, he walked across the room and closed the door. The green ball was still there. He pulled the shade down and drew the curtain closed. The glowing ball in the corner didn't change. He threw a blanket over the curtain that was over the shade. The light remained.

By this time, I knew the green glow wasn't coming from any light source. Pulling the covers a little tighter around me, I told him I thought the light was probably the ghost.

"A what?" he asked.

"A ghost. You know we have a ghost ... right?"

Apparently, he knew no such thing. I assumed he knew about ghosts and he assumed he hadn't married "a crazy woman." With the threat of hypothermia closing in on him, he finally gave up his quest and came to bed. "A ghost," he mumbled as he rolled over and went to sleep.

Day three of our marriage and I'd just discovered that I'd married a skeptic ... and we lived in a haunted house ... what fun.

2: FIRST YEAR

1985

....

Our house now had the necessities like water and gas. But we soon realized that in order to turn our home into what we wanted it to become, we were going to have to do more than apply a fresh coat of paint. The house needed a lot of work. Since it was our hope to stay here for the rest of our lives, we knew to make it right we needed to tear down what we had and start over one room at a time.

Wes and I were both working full time, so most of the remodeling took place on the weekends. Even so, everything about the house was beginning to change—new walls, new floors, and new windows. The only thing that remained the same was the green glowing ball of light that showed up in the corner of our bedroom every night. It was still there, night after night and week after week.

Wes tried everything to figure out what caused this light to appear. It had become his nightly mission. We'd go to bed and within a few minutes he'd be up "looking for the source." He'd eventually give up for the night, but on his way to bed he'd say, "There has to be a logical explanation."

I'd tell him there was a logical explanation. It was a ghost and she was probably laughing at him by this point.

Since we moved into this house with its weird little green glowing ball, I decided to ask around and get some other opinions about ghosts. To my surprise, I found out that Wes was in the majority. Apparently, sane-thinking adults didn't believe in ghosts. Where that left me, I wasn't so sure.

The only thing I was sure about was that living with a ghost was making me curious about them. I'd always believed, but now it was different, it was personal. My quest to learn more wasn't an easy one. Asking others hadn't worked out too well, and twenty-seven years ago, we didn't have access to the Internet or shows that dealt with the subject of ghosts. The shows that were available were fiction and marketed as such. I wasn't sure what to do other than observe what went on in our home.

Other than hearing footsteps, seeing the green glow each night, and feeling like someone was always watching me, there wasn't much to observe. I never thought about taking pictures and I'd never heard of an EVP (Electronic Voice Phenomena).

Wes and I rarely talked about the ghost anymore. He made it clear that he didn't believe in them and it made him uncomfortable to think I did. After months of his bedtime routine of trying to figure out where the light was coming from, he'd finally given up. I guess you could say he learned to live peacefully with the light. He learned to ignore it and I learned to treasure it.

Meanwhile, our house remodel continued. After a particularly successful weekend of demolition, I came home from work one Monday to discover that something about the house had changed. I felt it the minute I walked through the door. The house felt heavy. I wasn't sure what was going on, but I knew something wasn't quite right.

I walked through the house and everything looked the same as I'd left it that morning, but it didn't feel the same. I went into the room where we'd torn out the sheet-rock the day before and an overwhelming sense of sadness struck me. Then, I suddenly understood.

The ghost was upset. We were tearing up her home and she didn't like it one bit. Looking at the mess, I could understand why. What had once been a bedroom was now nothing more than bare studs. I wasn't sure what to do, so I did what I do best and started talking. I explained how we were trying to fix the house and I asked her to be patient with us. As I walked through the house, I could feel her walking alongside me. I started pointing out different things as I told her about all of our remodeling plans. Once we completed the tour, the heaviness lifted and the house felt normal again. As I sat down on the edge of the bed I thought, *Maybe I really am crazy. I just talked to a ghost.*

This experience was unlike anything I'd ever had before and I couldn't get it out of my head. I wanted—no—I *needed* to tell someone. Even though I knew Wes didn't believe in ghosts, I thought my experience might make him reconsider his stance. I was wrong. To him, ghosts simply didn't exist and the subject didn't warrant further consideration.

Being newlyweds, we knew there were going to be things we didn't agree on; apparently, the subject of ghosts was going to be one of them. I couldn't understand how it was possible for him not to believe. He, on the other hand, couldn't understand how I did. We were convinced that we each were right and we finally had to agree to disagree.

Even though I disagreed with his point of view concerning ghosts, after our talk, I at least understood where it came from.

Wes grew up on the same land where we now live, which is located next to a cemetery. Growing up, he heard family and friends talk about how they could never live there for fear of ghosts. As most parents would, his assured him ghosts did not exist.

This teaching grew in his mind. After all, according to the movies, if one was going to have a run-in with a ghost, the cemetery was the perfect place for that to happen and it never had.

Living where he did opened the door for discussion about ghosts in his childhood home, whereas I'd never questioned my own parents on the subject. As he learned through his parents that ghosts didn't exist, I'd learned through my own encounters that they did.

Wes made his feelings clear. Believing in ghosts was something reserved for children. I vowed to myself never to bring up the subject again.

3: GROWING FAMILY

1986–1989

....

Even though I no longer talked about the ghost, it didn't mean she wasn't around. After two years of marriage, I was now enjoying being a stay-at-home mom and the ghost was more active than ever. After we brought our newborn daughter Keshia home from the hospital, the green glowing ball now appeared during the day and in different rooms of the house. This was something new. Before, I had only seen the light at night and always in that one corner of our bedroom. I felt the ghost changed her routine so she could be around the baby.

Having lived with this entity for awhile now, I never had any thoughts of her hurting our daughter. As strange as it may sound, I'd come to think of the ghost as part of the family...a grandma of sorts. I knew she wasn't my grandma, but I was certain she'd been someone's at one time, and seeing the green glowing ball somehow brought me comfort.

But after a few months, I no longer saw the green ball during the day. She seemed to have settled back into her old way of doing things and only appeared at night.

Keshia's nursery was in our old bedroom; we had re-modeled another room to serve as our bedroom. These two rooms were connected. When I got up during the night to check on Keshia, it came as no surprise to see the green glow hovering in the same corner where we had first seen it. After all, that had always been her spot. What did come as a surprise was watching the green ball come around the corner on the nights I brought Keshia into our room. Apparently, I wasn't the only one who wanted to keep a watchful eye on the baby.

Two short years after having our daughter, we were blessed once again. This time our little bundle of joy was a boy. We put our son Troy in the nursery and moved Keshia into another bedroom. Once we did this, the green ball moved from room to room. When I'd get up in the night to check on the children, sometimes I'd see the green glow in Keshia's room, while at other times I'd see it in Troy's.

With our family expanding, it was becoming obvious we needed a bigger house. We decided to not only add on to our home, but to double it in size. We were going to add on a big living room, another bedroom, another bathroom, and an office. As exciting as the addition was, it was also loud. Day in, day out, there was the constant sound of construction. After a few weeks, it began taking its toll. The children were tired and cranky and I had a constant headache. To escape the noise, the kids and I spent our days at the park or at my sister Tammy's house.

After one of our all-day excursions, we came home to find the carpenters had left for the day and our home was blessedly quiet. Knowing the children were hungry, I put Troy in his high chair and Keshia at the table. With my back turned to them, I started making snacks. There was a loud bang. I whirled around and expected to see the high chair turned over or some other type of catastrophe mothers learn to expect.

To my relief, both of the children were sitting right where I'd put them. Troy had a startled expression and the beginnings of a pout forming on his little face. Keshia, however, was looking down the hall laughing while covering her ears.

After consoling Troy, I walked down the hall to see what could have made the noise. First, I noticed Keshia's bedroom door was closed. I generally left the doors open because it was summertime and we only had one air conditioning unit to cool the house. Just as I was about to open her door, Troy's door slammed shut.

I went into each one of the rooms to see if the windows were closed. They were. Knowing the construction crew hadn't worked on that side of the house, I couldn't come up with any reason as to why these two doors would suddenly slam shut. It had never happened before. I left their doors open, took one last look, and walked back toward the kitchen. Before I completed the short walk, Keshia's door slammed shut again. I wondered if our ghost had learned a new trick and if she was getting back at me for leaving her there to deal with all of the noise.

With our home frequently being in some state of remodel, I'd come to learn it wasn't unusual for the activity to pick up when we were working on the house. It was common to have missing hammers and paintbrushes turn up where we knew we hadn't put them. Apparently, hiding things wasn't enough now. She must have liked her new door-closing trick because she did it a lot. Thankfully, she'd learned to be quieter about it, but because of our squeaky hinges, it was still quite effective.

When we'd sit down at the table for dinner, the doors would slowly creak closed. The slow, drawn-out screech made an eerie sound. A sound even Wes had trouble ignoring. He'd look at me from across the table and say something about needing to oil the hinges.

I'd shrug and tell him that might help with the squeaking, but it wouldn't help with the doors opening and closing on their own. I didn't have to mention the ghost for him to know what I was thinking. He'd shake his head, smile, and tell me he'd fix the doors.

The game we'd gotten in the habit of playing was very frustrating to me. I knew we had a ghost and I was tired of him not acknowledging it. True, I was home more than he was, which allowed me more opportunities to see things—but he lived here too. He had to know that the things going on in our home were not normal.

4: CONFIRMATION

1990

....

I didn't have anyone I could talk to about the ghosts and the things I was experiencing, which left me feeling very frustrated. I longed to share these encounters with someone, but who? I'd learned the hard way this wasn't something you could talk about with just anyone. From my experiences, people either thought I was crazy, or even worse, thought I was lying. Not liking the options, I kept quiet.

Since I never mentioned our ghost to anyone, I was stunned one morning when, during a routine phone call, my sister Wanda asked me if I believed in ghosts.

I remember stammering into the phone. "What ... ? What did you say?"

She asked me again if I believed in ghosts. I had to pull up a chair as I tried to figure out where this question had come from. She went on to explain that she'd seen a show the night before about a couple who claimed their house was haunted.

I assumed she was referring to a fictional program. Trying to keep the disappointment from my voice, I asked her if she'd watched a horror movie or something.

She then explained the show was "supposedly" true.

She had my attention! My pulse raced. *A real haunting.* I tried to act calm as I asked her to tell me about the show.

"They claim," she emphasized the word "claim" to the point I could envision her rolling her eyes, "that things move by themselves and they can hear people walking around and stuff."

Refilling my coffee cup, I tried to keep my voice calm as I asked her if she believed in ghosts.

She said something to the effect that she wasn't sure, but that the show made her wonder. As exciting as it was to hear her say that, it was her next statement that really got to me. When she started talking about these "balls of light" that the show referred to as "orbs," I had to remind myself to breathe.

Balls of light! I had kept the fact that we had a ghost quiet for so long now, I couldn't contain myself. "Wanda!"

I blurted. "We have one of those! We have this green glowing ball; it's about the size of—"

"What?" she shrieked.

Wanda, being the older sibling, was not only used to being the protector, but she was accustomed to giving out orders she expected to be followed. In her controlled, don't-even-think-about-defying-me voice, she demanded that if I was serious she wanted me to "get out of that house ... now!"

For someone who wasn't sure if she believed in ghosts or not, she had quite a reaction. To be honest, she had me a little nervous by this point. I began to wonder what it was they had said on the show about these orbs. Were these orbs evil ... or ... what?

She told me that, according to this show, a ghost sometimes manifested itself in the form of orbs. She waited for my response. Not getting one, she asked if I had understood her. She clarified by telling me this orb could mean I had a ghost in my house.

Could have? I could tell the idea of me having a ghost wasn't sitting too well with her, so I tried to calm her by explaining that the green ball had always been here. That didn't help matters. I reminded her we'd lived here for over six years and nothing bad had ever happened. She didn't care. Wearing her big-sister hat, she made it clear she wanted me to leave the house immediately.

Laughing, I told her she was overacting and I couldn't just leave—this was our home. When she questioned me about my kids and told me I was putting them in danger, I regretted ever telling her about the green glowing ball. This conversation wasn't going at all as I'd hoped and neither did the ones in the following days. She did at least believe me, but she didn't in any way share my thoughts that there wasn't anything to be afraid of. After realizing she was truly concerned for our safety, while also knowing there wasn't anything I could say to change her mind, I tried to downplay it the best I could.

She wasn't buying it. She still wanted me to leave.

Even though I desperately wanted someone to talk with about the things going on in our home, I didn't think scaring my sister half to death was worth it. With a downtrodden spirit, I finally managed to choke out the words, "Just forget about it. It was probably my imagination."

As disappointing as it was to be back to having no one to talk to about our ghost, I had at least learned about the new show pertaining to true hauntings. The show was to air weekly and I not only started watching it, but eventually talked Wes into watching it with me. He still didn't believe in ghosts, but realizing I wasn't the only one who did somehow made me seem a little less crazy.

One evening after watching the show, Wes brought up the topic of the green glowing ball we "used" to see at night. Since I was a stay-at-home mom, he hadn't had the responsibilities of getting up with the children, so he apparently hadn't seen the green ball since we'd moved our bed into a different room.

Continuing our conversation, Wes commented on how the "nuts" hosting this show would have had a field day if they could've seen that ball. He readily admitted how "that thing" had almost driven him crazy as he tried to figure out what it was. Laughing, he said, "I wonder what made that thing finally go away?"

When I told him it hadn't gone anywhere, and that it was still around, he raised a skeptical brow and dropped the subject. With him using the term "nuts" to describe the hosts of the paranormal show, I knew he hadn't changed his mind about ghosts, but I couldn't help but notice his new interest in checking on the children before he went to bed at night.

5: OUR GREEN GHOST

1993

....

Keshia's friend Cindy spent many Friday nights at our house. One Saturday morning, I got up early to make the expected cherry turnovers for breakfast and I was surprised to see my seven-year-old daughter and her friend sleeping in the living room. After calling everyone to the table, I asked the two girls why they'd slept in the living room instead of in Keshia's room. Keshia giggled and told me that Cindy was afraid of our green ghost.

Those three words, "our green ghost" sent my pulse racing. I wasn't quite sure how to handle this situation. I only replied with an uneasy, "Oh yeah?"

"Yeah," Keshia said, as Cindy's little head bobbed up and down in complete agreement.

From across the table, Wes was looking at me as if to say, "What have you done?"

I responded to his look with a shake of my head. I'd never brought up the subject of ghosts to either of my children, but there it was, laid out in front of me, brought up by one of them, in front of company no less. Getting up from the table while pretending to be busy, the words "our green ghost," bounced around in my head. *Keshia knew about the ghost! Of course, she knew about her. Troy probably did too. Why wouldn't they? The ghost had been with us since before either of them were born.*

After breakfast, Cindy's dad came to pick her up. While I was busying myself with the breakfast cleanup, I casually asked Keshia if she really thought we had a ghost.

She looked at me with her big innocent eyes, as only a child can, and said "Duh! Our green ghost."

Wes seemed to deflate right in front of me. Ignoring him for the moment, I continued to ask Keshia about this green ghost as Wes sat quietly. I asked her if she, like Cindy, was ever afraid of the ghost.

She assured me she wasn't. She went on to tell me the green ghost was nice and that "she" was her friend.

She? It was then I asked her what the ghost looked like.

Keshia seemed confused; she asked me if I'd not ever seen her. Then she told me that "most of the time" the ghost was just a green ball.

Most of the time? I told her yes, I'd seen the green ball. I then asked her what she meant by "most of the time."

Her reply was that sometimes the green ball had a face and that was why Cindy got scared.

A face! I'd never seen a face in the green ball. *WOW!* I may have gotten a little scared myself if I'd seen that.

Validation—that's exactly what I was feeling—validation through a seven-year-old. Someone else finally got it. I wasn't crazy. We really did have a ghost. Not only did Keshia acknowledge we had a ghost, she knew it was a female, and she knew there wasn't any reason to be afraid of her. I could hardly believe my own ears. I decided to take my daughter's lead and put to rest the idea that I shouldn't discuss these experiences. She readily accepted the fact we had a ghost, which reinforced my theory that people believe in ghosts if they have an experience before they are "taught better." I stepped out on a limb and asked Troy if he'd ever seen the green ball.

After he confirmed that he'd seen it, I asked him if he thought it was a ghost. He shrugged. "Nope, it's just a ball."

So much for my theory.

That single conversation set the stage for many years to come. Keshia and I both believed in ghosts, Wes and Troy didn't. Both of them had seen the green ball, but it wasn't a ghost. No further explanation, it just wasn't a ghost.

I was determined not to have Keshia feel the way I'd felt for so many years. I didn't want her to think there was something wrong with her for believing in ghosts. I knew it would be important to keep the lines of communication open and let her know she could talk about the ghost if she wanted to. However, I did tell her she needed to be careful about telling everyone. I explained that, like Cindy, some people were scared of ghosts.

She took it all in stride and simply said, "Okay."

After Wes and I had the chance to talk alone later that night, he surmised the only "logical explanation" was Keshia must have overheard me talking to someone about the fact that I thought we had a ghost.

That seemed reasonable enough. The problem was that I knew I hadn't said anything like that around Keshia. I rarely spoke of the ghost, and never in front of the children, but that was going to change.

I didn't want the topic of ghosts to seem like a big deal to Keshia, so I gave it a few days before approaching the subject again. When I did bring it up, I asked her if she could remember the first time she'd ever seen the ghost.

Thinking about the question, she told me the ghost had always been here, but that she could remember when she was "little" how the ghost had taught her not to be afraid of thunderstorms.

I tried to act as though this was a typical conversation between a mother and child. I calmly asked her how the ghost had accomplished that.

Keshia wrinkled her forehead in thought and told me about a time when she was supposed to be taking a nap. She said that right after she laid down, it started to storm. When she heard a loud clap of thunder, she came and asked me if I'd lie down with her. Apparently, I was busy doing something, so I told her to get back in bed and I'd be there in a little while.

Keshia put her hands on her hips and said, "But you never came and I was still scared. That's when the ghost made me not scared."

My thoughts raced. *Did you see her? Did she talk to you? Did she touch you?* I had so many questions. Reminding myself to act casual, I settled for, "How did she make you not scared?"

"She let me look at the lightning and it was pretty."

I concentrated on keeping my voice steady as I asked her if the ghost had said anything to her.

She shook her head and told me the ghost didn't talk to her; the ghost just let her look at the lightning and it helped her not be afraid.

With my head reeling, I asked her what made her think the ghost was a girl.

Without giving it a second thought she said, "She's just a girl. Like me and you. But she's old, kind of like Grandma."

Exactly. Kind of like Grandma.

6: A NEW VENTURE

1994

....

Even though Wes and I didn't agree on the subject of ghosts, there was one thing we did agree on. Family came first—always. Wes was a talented trim carpenter and an accomplished furniture/cabinet builder. He had a good job, but it was a one-hundred-mile round trip and the company he worked for required massive amounts of overtime. Typically, he left before the children got up in the mornings and didn't make it home until after they'd gone to bed at night. When our six-year-old son started to ask when his daddy was going to come and visit, we knew it was time for a change.

Knowing the company Wes worked for subbed some of their work out to other companies, we began to entertain the idea of starting our own business. At first, I thought this was just one of those things couples dreamed about doing one day. Without realizing what I was getting into, I played along with the idea and said if he really wanted to do this, I'd work with him to help get the business started. Before I knew what was happening, we were out searching for a building we could rent. With my head spinning, we put a deposit down on a shop that was only five miles from our home and we began the exciting venture of starting our own business. The building had been empty for awhile, so when Wes went to purchase the equipment we were going to need, I stayed behind to clean the shop and get the office set up.

The first day I worked alone, I kept feeling as though someone else was there. This feeling was different from what I'd experienced at home. This was creepy. I didn't really sense I was in any danger, but I didn't like the feeling either. I walked through the building and checked each room. There was no one there but me. For peace of mind, I locked the door before I started cleaning the back part of the shop.

As I swept the floors, I tried to convince myself that I simply got spooked by being in an unfamiliar place by myself. With my head down and my mind focused on what I was doing, the lights went off, then came back on. I jerked my head up and saw what I thought was Wes standing in the shadows of the doorway. I yelled out to him not to do that.

I made my way across the long shop and told him he'd made it back earlier than I thought he would. Still walking to the door, I asked if he'd already gotten everything he needed. He never answered. I made my way to the front of the shop, but couldn't find him anywhere. I walked over to the window and looked outside for his truck. It wasn't there. A cold chill ran down my spine as I looked back at the empty doorway where I'd seen someone standing seconds before.

I didn't want to go back into the shop area, so I turned off the lights and shut the door. I decided to work up front and get the office ready. I started organizing the file cabinet. As I dropped the crisp, new folders into place, I couldn't shake the feeling that someone was standing behind me, looking over my shoulder. Trying to ignore it, I sat down at the desk and put a piece of paper into the typewriter. Whoever it was seemed to have backed away a little, but they were still there—watching.

After working a few days by myself and dealing with the feeling of always being watched, I started to complain to Wes about not wanting to be there alone. He hadn't been impressed when I told him our house was haunted and he sure wasn't impressed when I told him I thought the shop was, too.

Even though he didn't put much stock in my complaints, he agreed to try to minimize the time I had tospend there alone. If Wes and I were both there, I could still feel the presence of what I now believe to be an older man, but as long as I wasn't alone, the feeling was tolerable. Of course, to Wes, it was nothing more than my overactive imagination.

If it was my imagination, Wes soon got a healthy dose of "imagination," too. With the business now in full operation, he'd go to work at the shop in the morning while I got the children off to school. After dropping them off, I'd walk into the shop and announce, "I'm here."

Without fail, he'd jump, and then scream, "Why do you do that?"

At first, I thought it was kind of funny, but after awhile I got tired of being yelled at. Trying to have a calmer start to the workday, I walked in one morning and stood perfectly still until he noticed I was there. That was a bad idea. He actually threw a tool across the shop that morning.

Wes had never been an overly skittish person, but he was sure becoming one. I was constantly asking him why he was so jumpy and what I could do to prevent scaring him when I came into work.

He'd laugh it off and tell me that maybe I should wear bells or something. Keeping that in mind, I walked in one morning, picked up the office phone, dialed our own number, and hung up. Knowing our phone would ring, I sat at the desk and waited for him to come and answer it. When he came through the door, I said, "It's just me."

He jumped straight up and literally spun around in the air. Before his feet hit the ground, he was yelling.

Even though I hadn't meant to scare him, I couldn't help but laugh. Trying to control myself, I asked him again how he would like me to come into work, because nothing I tried seemed to be acceptable.

Now laughing himself, he admitted there was nothing different for me to try. We were just going to have to accept the fact that I would start my workday by being yelled at, while he started his with having the bejabbers scared out of him.

Even though Wes wouldn't even entertain the idea that the shop could be haunted, he too started to complain that he always felt as though someone were watching him. When I questioned him about it, he'd say, "This is just a creepy old building." He also talked about how my wild imagination must have been getting to him. I didn't think my imagination had anything to do with it, nor did it have anything to do with what happened next.

7: TUCKER

1995

. . . .

Wes and I soon learned that talking about starting a business was much easier than actually doing it. Before long, we were working ten-, twelve-, and sometimes fourteen-hour days, usually six days a week. This hadn't been in our plans, but there didn't seem to be too much we could do about it.

Putting in so many hours, we had to stop and remind ourselves why we started the business to begin with. Wes had wanted to spend more time with the kids, but now we were both gone. None of us were too happy with the way things were turning out. Not having a choice about the hours we had to work, our solution was to make a play area for the kids so they could come to the shop after school. It wasn't the ideal situation, but we could at least all be together.

Since we rarely used the office, we converted it into the TV room. We hooked up the child-mandatory Nintendo game system and brought in two beanbag chairs. We turned the front section of the shop into their personal skating rink and converted the attic into a large playroom. Even though the kids had a better play area at the shop than they did at home, they complained about being bored. Trying to make the shop feel more like home, we agreed to let them bring their dog, Tucker, to the shop.

On the first day, Tucker jumped into the back of the truck ready for whatever the kids had in store for him. Pulling into the shop's drive, the three of them leapt out, ready for their new adventure. After we let Tucker check out the property, we all went inside. Tucker walked into the shop a few feet and abruptly stopped. Refusing to go any further, he stuck his tail between his legs and started to whine.

We'd all seen this before. At home, Tucker loved coming into the house, but there were certain areas he didn't like to go. These were the same areas that Keshia and I "claimed" our ghost generally occupied.

We tried to coax Tucker further into the shop. He wouldn't budge. The kids finally decided they would take him outside to play Frisbee. Wes and I went to work.

Checking on them a little later, I found them all in the office watching TV. Whatever had bothered Tucker earlier obviously wasn't bothering him now. He seemed perfectly content serving as the children's pillow in front of the television.

I'd been back to work only for a little while when Troy asked me to come and check on Tucker. When I opened the door to the front section of the shop, I heard him whimpering. He was lying on the floor next to the break room; right where I'd once seen the apparition that I mistook for Wes.

I tried to pull Tucker to his feet and he howled out as if he were in pain. Both the kids said he was fine until they went into the break room to get a snack. When the kids walked out of the break room, Tucker jumped up, ready to follow them. When they turned and went back into the break room, Tucker plopped down by the door and started the sorrowful howling once again.

Wes could hear all the noise from the back part of the shop. He came in to see what the commotion was about. We showed him how Tucker responded when the kids came out of the break room and how he acted when they went back in. Not knowing what else to do, we got a piece of bologna and tried to get him to come into the break room with us. When he refused the bologna, we knew something was definitely wrong. Keshia asked me if I thought Tucker was afraid of the ghost. That was exactly what I was thinking, but Wes said something about this being ridiculous and he bent down and picked the dog up.

Tucker was a full-grown Labrador and was quite a handful. When Wes tried to walk through the doorway, Tucker put his front paws on both sides of the jamb. It was quite a struggle for Wes to get Tucker's legs out of the way so they could make it through the door. When they got into the room, Wes sat down on the floor and tried to console Tucker.

I had never seen Tucker act this way before. At home, there were places he didn't want to go, but he'd never reacted like this. His tail remained tucked and his eyes shone with fear as he shook and whimpered. The minute Wes let go of him, he jumped to his feet, skidded across the floor, and ran out the door.

Most people accept the fact animals have some type of extrasensory perception. Before technology advanced to the point it is today, people commonly watched animals to predict changes in the weather. Today there are studies that show how an animal's behavior changes before earthquakes and some are even thought to be able to detect seizures in patients suffering from epilepsy.

The theories as to why they are able to detect certain things vary greatly. Some claim these abilities come from their keen sense of smell and their ability to detect minor changes that people cannot. Others think animals have a natural sixth sense. However they are able to accomplish these things, many people also think this ability allows them to detect the presence of ghosts. Since Tucker had strong reactions to places where I'd had personal experiences, I think this theory is worth considering.

1996–1998

....

After a year of owning our own business, finances necessitated I return to work outside of our company for a while. Since Wes's schedule was now more flexible than mine was, he was the one in charge of watching the children after school. Being the ages of ten and eight, they didn't need a lot of supervision and by this time, they had a good setup at the shop. If the TV room and the "skating rink" failed to entertain them, they still had the attic that we'd converted into the playroom. The attic was where I usually found them when I got off work and picked them up. Of all of their choices, that seemed to be their favorite place to play. I never understood their attraction to the attic until a few years later.

After we had rented the building for a couple of years, we decided to build a shop of our own next to the house. After moving into the new building, I overheard the children talking one day about how they missed the old shop. This came as a surprise to me, but now having some experience at being a mother I'd learned the best way to find out what was going on with the kids was to listen to them as they talked to each other.

"I liked the old shop better," Troy said as he and Keshia came in to set the table for dinner. "I kind of miss it."

"Yeah, me too, the new shop isn't any fun. Dad won't even let us skate in there."

Troy slammed the plate down on the table. "I know. It stinks!"

I thought I must've heard something wrong when Troy said he wondered what the spool was doing and that they should have asked their dad if they could bring it to the new shop.

I knew what he meant by "spool," but I didn't know why he would want it. Two empty utility spools had been left behind by whomever had used the building prior to us renting it. We'd turned one of them up on its end and converted it into a table for the kids to use. Instead of trying to haul the other one down the stairs, we'd left it lying in the corner of the attic.

My ears really perked up when I heard them talking about how the spool would chase them. I turned off the stove, went into the dining room, and asked them what they were talking about.

Putting the silverware down beside the plates, Troy told me one of the spools used to chase them around the attic.

I laughed and said something about that being impossible.

Keshia, now being a little older, contemplated the absurdity of it all. She told me she didn't know how the spool was able to chase them, but that it really had.

I sat down at the table and tried to remember where the spool was the last time I'd paid attention to it. I commented on how it must have been on an incline or something.

Keshia shook her head as she told me that couldn't have been the reason because the spool had chased them back and forth throughout the attic. She shrugged. "I think the ghost just liked playing with us."

Troy rolled his eyes and voiced his complaints about Keshia believing in ghosts. He agreed that there was something "weird" about that spool, but it had nothing to do with ghosts.

Even though dinner was getting cold, I knew I wanted to hear more of this story. After talking with the kids for awhile, I too had my suspicions that this activity was brought on by the ghost that haunted the old shop. They

told me that sometimes when they were in the attic playing, the spool would slowly start moving towards them.
They would get in front of it and run to the wall. The
spool would then stop, let them walk around it, and then
chase them to the other end.

Wes came into the house and saw all of us sitting
around the foodless table. "Isn't it time to eat?" he asked.

I waved him to a chair and told him we'd eat in a little
while, but I wanted him to hear some things the kids were
telling me about the old shop.

After getting him caught up with the conversation,
he shook his head and replied that there was no possible
way the spool could move on its own—at least not back
and forth.

When Keshia commented on how she thought it was
the ghost, Wes sighed. "And here we go again."

Keshia asked him that if the shop wasn't haunted,
how would he explain why she and Troy were locked in
the attic all of the time.

Wes exhaled as if someone had just hit him in the
stomach. He sat back hard in his chair and mumbled
something about how he'd forgotten about that.

Now I was confused. I had no idea what they were
talking about. Wes sat quietly and listened as both of the
kids filled me in.

Apparently, when the kids were in the attic playing, it
wasn't unusual for them to find that they were locked in.
They would have to go over to the window that looked

out into the shop and yell until they could get their dad's attention. Wes confirmed that when he'd get to the attic door, he'd find that it had been locked—from the outside.

I couldn't believe what I was hearing. The door that led to the attic was a hatch door that had to be pushed open from the stairs. The lock was only accessible from the stairs. If the kids were in the attic and Wes was in the shop... Who could have locked the door?

Trying to process all of this was giving me a headache. I was having trouble understanding how this could happen and why no one ever stopped to think about how the door got locked. "Wes," I said, looking at him in disbelief.

He put his hands up in the air, "I don't know." He went on to say that those were hard times and he honestly hadn't given it much thought. He said he'd open the door and tell them to quit bothering him.

I was stunned and couldn't believe he'd never thought about it. As I voiced my dissatisfaction in the care he'd given the kids, I could see that Troy was enjoying seeing his dad get "in trouble." Wanting to see a little more, he started mimicking Wes's response. He poked at the air with his index finger. "I'm busy, you two quit fooling around or I'm going to make it to where you can't play up there anymore."

After laughing at Troy's performance, Wes said, "I don't know how that door kept getting locked all the time, but it sure did."

I'd always known that old building was haunted, but I had no idea of the amount of activity that had gone on there. Once I started working outside the shop, I rarely went there other than to pick up the kids. Now I was beginning to wonder what I'd missed.

Pulling me back from my thoughts, Keshia relayed another "game" to me that she used to play in the attic. She said she'd take a handful of crayons and drop them on the table. She'd pick a color and ask her invisible playmate to move it. After she'd gone through each color, she'd start over, but this time asking the ghost to drop them to the floor. Keshia would watch as the crayon she'd specified would roll across the table and land on the floor.

When Keshia and Troy were young, and trying to learn their colors, I played this game with them. Why Keshia decided to play this game with a ghost could be anyone's guess. But growing up with a ghost in her own home somehow made the ghost's response seem normal—it was, after all, a two-person game and she needed a partner.

1998

....

I wasn't seeing the green ghost as often as I once had. Mostly because in the course of four years, I went from being a stay-at-home mom, to working with Wes, to re-joining the medical field, and then back to working with Wes again. My schedule was crazy and I was rarely home. However, when I cut my hours to part time, I still wasn't seeing the green ghost regularly. Weeks would go by without me noticing any activity, then the weeks turned into months. Sometimes I wasn't even sure if she was still with us at all.

fourteen years and her being here just felt right. Somehow, she completed our family and I felt as though she belonged with us.

Then one day I was rushing through the house gathering up a load of laundry when I walked right past her—not the familiar green glowing ball—but *the woman*. At first, my brain didn't comprehend what I had seen. I'd walked right behind her. Then it registered. As soon as I made the step down out of the dining room, it hit me: the green ghost! I spun around just in time to watch her vanish. She was there one second and then she was gone.

I stopped and stared at the now-empty dining room. I don't know how I knew it was her, but I did. "Hello," I stammered. "Are you here?" My trembling voice was the only noise in the room.

The woman that had come to mean so much to me had been standing right there in the dining room. I couldn't believe it. I played the short scene over and over in my mind as I tried to recall every detail. She was wearing what I'd describe as a green, tapestry dress. She was short and a little on the heavy side. She had the most beautiful white hair and it was done up in a pin-curl bun. She'd been standing there looking at a picture of my grandma that I had hanging on the wall.

As I stared at the spot where she'd stood, I tried to make sense out of what had happened. *After all these years, why hadn't I ever seen her in that way before? Why now? What did it all mean?* I didn't have any answers—only more questions.

Thinking of nothing else that day, I couldn't wait to tell the rest of the family. As soon as everyone got home, I announced they weren't going to believe what happened to me that day. Having everyone's attention, I told them I had seen the green ghost.

Wes and Troy exchanged their "Yep, she's crazy" look with one another.

Refusing to be discouraged, I told them I was being serious and that I hadn't just seen the green ball, but the woman herself.

Keshia interrupted my ramblings by saying she'd forgotten to mention it, but that she thought she had seen her too.

I was stunned. *Forgot! How could she forget something like that?* Seeing the woman standing there had been a significant experience for me, and one I'd never forget. I guess that's the difference in having always lived with a ghost. To Keshia it was a "cool experience," but in the scheme of things, it wasn't that big of a deal. To me it was a big deal—a very big deal. When I was finally able to find my voice, I asked Keshia to tell me about her experience.

With Wes and Troy sitting quietly, Keshia said that a few days before, she thought she had seen the green ghost through the window. Keshia said she had been out on the porch getting ready to come in the house when she saw a woman standing in the dining room looking at my grandma's picture.

Looking at my grandma's picture! I asked her to describe what the woman looked like.

Keshia reiterated that she'd only seen her through the window, but she thought the woman was short. She went on to say the woman was wearing a green dress and she had pretty white hair.

Keshia had just described exactly what I'd seen. The woman had the same physical description. She was in the same spot, and doing the same thing. Since Keshia and I had both seen her looking at my grandma's picture, I kept wondering what the significance of that might have been. Since I didn't know who the green ghost was, it was impossible for me to know if there was any connection between her and my grandma. My grandma had passed away a few years earlier and after her death, I'd taken some crocheted doilies she'd made and put them in a frame along with her picture. For some reason the ghost seemed to be interested in this.

Throughout the conversation, Wes and Troy remained quiet. They knew it would be pointless to try to convince us we had not seen the green ghost, just as Keshia and I knew we couldn't convince them we had.

We didn't realize it at the time, but later Keshia and I came to feel that was the green ghost's way of saying good-bye. After we'd both seen her in the dining room, we never again witnessed that peculiar green glowing ball of light nor did we ever "feel" that loving watchful eye on us again.

After a time of not seeing her, we realized that she truly was gone. To me, it was almost as if we'd lost a family member. Personally, I've never again connected with any of our ghosts as I did with her. That's not to say my opportunities were limited.

During the same time we noticed the green ghost was gone, Keshia and I also noticed we had a few new entities in our home. Up to this point, we'd always just had the green ghost, but that wasn't the case anymore. Just as I couldn't understand why she'd left, I didn't understand why we now had other entities. I sometimes said I thought the green ghost must've left the door open. In later years, I learned that maybe that wasn't so far from the truth.

There are many theories about why certain places may have ghostly activity. I think ghosts are more prevalent than most people think. In fact, I think they're very common. Like the rest of us, I think they just want acknowledgement. If they encounter someone who knows they are there, they tend to stick around, sometimes for a long, long time.

One of our new entities chose to make her presence known in an unusual way. One hot Sunday afternoon, we all decided to take a nap in the living room because it was the coolest room in the house. I was lying on the couch just about to drift off to sleep when I heard someone moving around in the kitchen. After hearing the water turn on and off in the kitchen, it finally got quiet and I went to sleep.

After I woke up, Wes asked me if I'd enjoyed my nap. I grumbled about how I would've enjoyed it a lot more if whoever was up making all of the noise would have been quiet. He seemed a little confused as he commented on how he'd thought I was the one making all the noise.

Still scowling, I turned to the children and asked which one of them was being so noisy. Before either of them could answer, Wes interjected, "And who watered the plant?"

With my mood showing no signs of improvement, I snapped at him that I was the only one who ever bothered to water the plants. I continued my rant by telling him if I left that up to anyone else, the plants would've all died years ago.

Wes looked at the kids as he stated again that someone had watered the plants.

I stomped over to check the plants. Wes was right, one of them was wet. I tried to gently slide off my high horse as I relented, sided with Wes, and asked the same question he had about who had watered the plant.

We all looked to Keshia, knowing that other than me she would be the most likely candidate to do something like that without being told. She met our stare and said it hadn't been her.

After hearing Troy also deny the accusations, I noticed water droplets trailing from the kitchen to the plants in the living room. Someone had obviously watered the plants—but who?

10: LOOK AT ME

1998

....

The green ghost that had shared our home had, for the most part, been content in fading into the background. If someone chose to ignore her presence, they could. The green glow was a little hard to get past sometimes, but the quiet footsteps and the creaking doors could easily be dismissed. But that wasn't the case with at least one of our new entities. Keshia and I both felt as though this ghost was male, and ignoring him wasn't going to be an easy option. He wanted attention and he knew how to get it.

When Troy was about ten years old, he had a run-in with this ghost that was hard to overlook. Troy was very close to my younger brother, Kevin, who was a bull rider. Kevin sent Troy two pictures of himself that had been taken during a recent bull ride. One picture showed Kevin on the back of a bull while the other picture showed him under it. Troy took great pride in displaying these pictures on his dresser.

One day after coming home from school, Troy complained to me that he kept finding Kevin's pictures on the floor. I was at home by myself during the day and I had no idea as to why his pictures would be on the floor. The only thing I could think of was maybe Troy had slammed his door before going to school, which might have caused the pictures to fall.

Despite Troy being mindful of how he closed his door, he continued to find the pictures on the floor. I never thought too much about it until one evening when I went into his room and I saw the pictures lying face down on his dresser. As I went to set them up, Troy yelled for me to stop.

I jerked my hand back and jumped away from the dresser. With the same urgent tone Troy had used, I yelled back and asked him what was wrong. He explained that every time he set the pictures up they'd fall to the floor again.

I thought that maybe the frame was faulty so I picked it up to look at it. Troy came over, took the picture from me, laid it face down on his dresser and asked me to leave it alone.

I thought his behavior was a little odd, but I did as he asked me to do. A few days later, I noticed the pictures weren't even on his dresser anymore. When I asked him about it, he said even though he'd kept them lying down, he continued to find them on the floor so he'd put them in a drawer.

At this point, I suspected something paranormal might be happening. Knowing how Troy felt about the subject of ghosts, I kept my feelings to myself. I knew the problems that came with believing in ghosts so I thought if Troy could continue to live in our house and not believe in them, I wouldn't interfere.

If I had any doubt about what was taking place in Troy's room, that doubt disappeared when Troy handed me the two pictures one day and asked me to put them away somewhere because he didn't want them anymore.

Knowing how he treasured these pictures, I asked him why he didn't want them. After shuffling his feet for a minute, he told me he'd been lying on his bed and one of the pictures had come out of his drawer, flown across the room, slammed against his closet door, and crashed to the floor.

Troy was a bit of a prankster, but seeing his anxious expression caused warning bells to go off in my head. My hands trembled as I took the pictures from him. I wasn't sure what to do. I was shocked ... and to be honest, a little scared. As he started to walk off, he told me he knew what I was thinking and this had nothing to do with ghosts.

Hmm, still not a ghost… okay.

Since Troy wasn't giving this ghost the attention he wanted, I guess the ghost decided to see if he'd have better luck in Keshia's room. Keshia had always been an excellent student and her bedroom held the evidence. Over the years, she'd received numerous medals and plaques honoring her for her academic achievements. She had most of these medals hanging on a pegboard in her room with the plaques hanging beside them.

The ghost was apparently fascinated with these medals and enjoyed playing with them. She said her pegboard would sometimes vibrate as if someone was shaking it and that, once in awhile, the pegboard would come out away from the wall then slam back with such force that some of the medals would fall to the floor.

I was never sure what to make of this ghost's behavior. All I could be sure of was that it was much more active than the ghost we'd had before. I can't say I was actually scared of him, but I was definitely leery of him. Keshia was more accepting; she seemed to view him more as an annoying brother. She didn't like him messing with her things, but she "tolerated" him, which I sometimes had trouble doing.

One day, Keshia and I were in her room talking when one of her plaques came off the wall, sailed across the room, and slammed into the opposite wall. While I jumped and screamed, Keshia was unruffled. She got up, picked up her plaque, and said, "Stop it, punk," and calmly tried to resume our conversation.

I didn't know whether I should laugh or cry. I was stunned, scared, and intrigued all at the same time. I asked her if she seriously just called the ghost a punk. She shrugged as she told me the ghost needed to learn to quit throwing her stuff.

I looked at where the plaque had hung compared to where it had landed. It was at least eight feet. I didn't know if ghosts were typically able to do this type of thing, but I knew I didn't like it. Knowing this was probably similar to the activity Troy had witnessed in his room made me fully understand his apprehension. With my anxiety building, I expressed my concerns about how the plaque could've hit her.

My twelve-year-old daughter first told me to calm down; she then went on to say if the ghost had wanted to hit her with the plaque, he would have. She ended with "Believe me, I know."

I tried to swallow my panic, and fearing I wasn't going to like the answer, I asked her what she meant by that statement.

She told me this hadn't been the first time the ghost had caused something to fly across her room. Keshia had kept a little metal Corvette on her dresser for years. She said the ghost had gotten to where he would throw the car at her and hit her in the head. She complained that even though the car couldn't have done any real damage to her, it did hurt. Her solution was to "hide" the car from the ghost by putting it in another room.

This story did nothing to make me feel better. Seeing my wide-eyed expression, she laughed and told me that it wasn't like the car could have killed her; the ghost just wanted attention.

Wanting attention was one thing, but this... I didn't like. I tried to talk to Wes about it, but the best he could muster was a pretense of "checking it out." True to his word, he went into Keshia's room and inspected the nail where the plaque hung. Finding nothing wrong with the nail, he pounded around on the wall, then put his ear up to it.

I didn't have a clue as to what he was doing. He claimed he was listening for bees. After hearing how the pegboard would sometimes vibrate, he thought bees might have built a nest in the wall. For once, I was impressed with one of his theories. A nest of bees wouldn't explain things flying through the air, but I could see the possibility of it causing the board to vibrate.

Failing to find evidence that bees or anything else had made their home in the walls, Wes gave up looking for the "logical explanation," which of course, to him, didn't mean one didn't exist. Not knowing what else to do, I settled for asking the ghost to stop—it didn't work.

The pegboard in Keshia's room was still the main attraction. The large two-by-three-foot board continued to shake and bounce, dropping medals to the floor in its wake.

Unrelated to these incidents, Keshia decided to rearrange her room. After changing things around we noticed the ghost seemed to have lost interest in her medals. I was relieved, but in a few months time she'd grown bored with the new arrangement and moved things back to where they'd previously been. Soon afterwards, the medals started slamming against the wall again, and on occasion a plaque would whiz by her head. Keshia's answer to this problem was simply to move the medals to a different place. She reasoned the ghost just didn't like them on that wall.

After Keshia moved the medals, the ghost again left them alone. For several years, Keshia wasn't "allowed" to put anything on that wall. If she did, it would mysteriously fall from the nail or sail across the room. It appeared this ghost had several quirks about how and where he liked things. He evidently didn't like Kevin's pictures in Troy's room, and he didn't like Keshia putting anything on that wall. I didn't realize it at the time, but he and I obviously had different ideas on the cabinet doors as well.

To my family's disappointment, I'm a very meticulous housekeeper. My motto is everything has its place and it should be put back there—always; no exceptions. One of my pet peeves is having the cabinet doors left open. It seemed as though I constantly repeated, "Close the cabinet doors when you're through." Yet, each time I went into the kitchen, they were open.

I knew in the scheme of things that it really wasn't that big of a deal. Then again, how hard was it to close a cabinet door? I continued to complain as each of them continued to deny they'd left the doors open. It never occurred to me that the culprit could have been a ghost.

One morning after taking the kids to school, I came home to find every cabinet door in the kitchen wide open. I was sure I hadn't left the house in that kind of shape. I shut each door, all the while wondering if I'd been complaining to the wrong people.

After I shut the doors, I went outside to do some yard work. I came back inside about thirty minutes later. I knew I had some apologizing to do. Once again, every door in the kitchen was wide open. No one else was home that morning—no one I could see anyway.

II: ELECTRIFYING NIGHT

1998

....

The different entities we'd encountered in our home had taught me to see them in much the same way as we see each other. I was learning that, like us, they each had their own unique personalities. With each passing incident, it was becoming easier to tell which ghost was doing what, but just when I thought I had it all figured out, a new ghost showed me I still had a few things to learn.

Every summer, Keshia and Troy attended a one-week session of church camp. Most years they were able to attend the same session, but because of their age difference, they occasionally had to attend separately. Being one such year, Wes and I decided to do something special with whichever child was left at home.

During Keshia's week to be "stuck with the parents," she chose to get dressed up and go out to a nice restaurant. At the time, Keshia was almost thirteen and I was beginning to see having a teenage daughter might not be so bad after all. I, for one, was enjoying her adultlike choices, with nothing involving video games, cold pizza, loud noise, or a ball pit.

I was getting ready to go out for dinner. After I got out of the shower, I headed to the bedroom outfitted in a fluffy towel. As I came through the living room, I saw Keshia sitting in the middle of the floor looking a little troubled. She asked me if I felt anything. I stopped to readjust my towel and told her I felt wet and half-naked.

She didn't find my answer amusing. She told me she was serious as she asked me again if I could feel anything. She said she didn't think we were alone. This wasn't an unusual topic between Keshia and me, but she seemed upset about it and that was unusual. I told her to hang on a minute and let me get my clothes on and I'd be right back. After getting dressed, I came back into the living room and saw Keshia still sitting in the middle of the floor. Something was definitely bothering her.

As I sat down on the couch, I noticed the air felt charged with electricity. The longer I sat there, the more ominous the feeling became. The air was heavy. Living in Oklahoma, I was familiar with what the air felt like when a storm was brewing. Looking out the window, I could see there wasn't a cloud in the sky. There was a storm developing all right, but it was in my living room.

When I asked her how long the room had felt this way, she said it had started as soon as I went to take a shower. She said she knew it was going to sound weird but she'd seen the shadow of a hand streak across the ceiling and then the room grew heavy. There was no denying that the air was heavy. It was actually getting hard to breathe. Keshia stood up, told me she couldn't take it anymore and that she was going outside to sit on the porch.

As soon as she went out, the heaviness left. I'd never experienced anything quite like this and I wasn't sure what to make of it. After sitting there for awhile, I reassured myself that whatever had been there was gone. Walking out to the porch, I told Keshia I thought everything was okay and we should go get ready for our night on the town.

When we went back into the house, we went into our own bedrooms to get ready. As I started to put on my makeup, my room filled with that same heaviness I'd felt earlier. I turned around and saw Keshia standing in my doorway. I started to wonder if this thing was following her around, and if so, why? I didn't want her to know of my suspicions until I could be sure. I tried to act casual as I told her again to go get ready. Once more, when she left, so did the heaviness.

I was feeling very uneasy about this ghost so I waited only a few minutes and called her back to my room. When she came in, the heaviness followed. I then told her I wasn't trying to scare her, but I thought whatever this thing was, it seemed to be following her. She agreed. She said the heaviness had followed her outside and to her room. Her lips trembled as she told me she couldn't get away from it.

Trying to sound braver than I felt, I told her I was sure it wasn't anything to worry about, but that we should probably stick together. She nodded as she sat down on my bed. Over the years we'd encountered so many different ghosts in our home that it had somehow become normal, but this was different and we both knew it. As we talked, the lights in my ceiling fan and the lights over my vanity started to flicker. These two lights are not only on separate switches, but they are also on separate circuits. Looking at Keshia, I knew the fear I saw on her face must have looked much like my own.

When the lights stopped flickering, I addressed the ghost. "Was that you?" There was no response. Keshia and I stared at one another as the silence hung in the air. I took a deep breath and tried again. "If that was you, make the lights flicker again." On cue, both sets of lights began to flicker. I bolted out of my chair and told Keshia we should probably wait in the living room for Wes to come home from work.

When we returned to the living room, the lights in there started to flicker. After a few minutes of sitting in silence, I asked Keshia if she was getting any feelings about this ghost. Usually one, if not both of us, would get impressions, which allowed us some insight as to who we were dealing with. Neither of us was receiving any information. That added to the level of fear, because we knew nothing about who this was or, more importantly, what it wanted.

When Wes pulled into the drive, Keshia and I jumped up and met him at the door. When he walked in, we greeted him with, "Let's go."

Keshia and I continued to crowd him in the entryway as he pushed past us to set his stuff down. "What's going on here? Are you two that hungry?"

It was all I could do at that point not to burst out in tears. I tried to remain calm as I asked him again if we could just go ahead and leave. When he complained about needing to take a shower, Keshia joined in and pleaded with him as well.

Looking back and forth between the two of us, he knew something wasn't right. With the stipulation that we'd tell him what was going on as soon as we left, he finally conceded, saying he'd forgo the shower, but that he at least needed to change his clothes.

After a quick change, we all loaded into the car. When the last door clicked shut, he asked what had caused us to be in such a rush. To his credit, he listened carefully as Keshia and I told him everything that had happened.

Even though Wes didn't believe in ghosts, seeing my and Keshia's reactions to the experience had him curious. Over the years, he'd heard us talk about different things we attributed to our ghosts, but he'd never known us to be scared of one, so he had a lot of questions. We continued to talk about the incident all the way to the restaurant. Arriving forty-five minutes later, it was Keshia and I who wanted to drop the subject and go on with our evening as planned. Trying to keep it from our thoughts, we managed to have a good time, but as we got closer to home, the tension started to build. As we pulled into the drive, we expressed our uneasiness about going into the house, but Wes was anxious to go "check it out."

The minute we walked into the house, I knew it was still there. The living room had that electrically charged feel to it. I went straight to my room on the pretense of putting my shoes and purse away. In truth, I was hoping to escape that awful feeling, but Wes, Keshia, and the heaviness all followed me. Wes stood in the center of our bedroom and looked around. I expected him to say something like, "see, there's nothing here," but to my surprise, he commented on how the air felt heavy. He surprised me again by addressing the ghost. When the bedroom lights started to flicker, Wes sank down on the edge of the bed.

Keshia and I had told him earlier how we thought the ghost was following her around, so we weren't surprised when he asked Keshia to go into another part of the house. When she left, the heaviness lifted.

Wes looked very surprised as he asked me if I'd felt the air change. He waited a few minutes and called Keshia back into our room. As she returned, so did the heavy feeling. He asked Keshia if she felt the heaviness go with her when she'd left. After she told him she could, he asked her to leave again. Just like before, when she left the room, so did the heavy feeling.

For the first time I wanted him—needed him—expected him, to tell me this was all in my head. He didn't. He felt it too, which did nothing to ease my fears. Unsure of himself, Wes looked at the ceiling and asked, "Is there anyone in here?" We heard Keshia yell that the lights were flashing.

Wes and I both ran to the sound of her voice. We found her standing in the bathroom. The lights weren't flickering, as in going off and on, but they would get very dim then go back to normal, then get dim again. Each time they dimmed, they emitted a buzzing sound.

Not knowing what else to do, we all went back to my and Wes's bedroom. Sitting there, Keshia and I finally started getting impressions of the ghost. "It's scared," I said.

"What?" Wes asked.

As the impressions flooded my mind, I told him I thought I'd had it all wrong. The ghost wasn't trying to scare us—he was scared.

"That's right," Keshia said. "He's scared. I think he has trouble understanding us, like maybe he speaks a different language."

At the same time, Keshia and I both said, "He's an Indian."

Wes was having a little trouble comprehending all of this. He knew Keshia and I "claimed" to receive impressions from ghosts, but he'd never experienced it before.

Keshia tried again to explain to Wes that we'd been wrong. She told him the ghost hadn't been trying to scare us, but that we had picked up on his fear and had misunderstood that for our own. I nodded my agreement when she told him the ghost was a young Indian, probably in his late teens or early twenties.

Wes didn't know what to think. He'd never experienced anything like this before. He'd felt the heaviness and he'd seen the flickering lights, but still...

Feeling better about the circumstances, Keshia told us she was going to get ready for bed. "Wait, wait, wait, and hold on a second." Wes said. Obviously, he wasn't feeling any better about the situation, at all. "I uh, I want to try and talk to this thing."

"Him," Keshia corrected.

"Okay, him." Wes cleared his throat. "Okay I'm going to ask you a few questions," he said to the ghost. "If you can understand me, I want you to make the lights flicker once for yes and twice for no. Is there someone in here?"

The light flickered once. Wes's eyebrows shot up. "Okay, are you an Indian?" The light again flickered once. "Are you a male?" Flicker. "Are you a female?" Flicker, flicker. "Have you been following Keshia around the house?" Flicker. "Do you plan to hurt her?" Flicker, flicker.

"Dad," Keshia laughed. "He's not going to hurt me, he just wants a friend."

No longer having any apprehensions about this ghost, Keshia went to bed while Wes and I stayed up discussing the events. Finally getting to bed ourselves, I'd hoped this encounter would help him come to terms with the fact that ghosts did exist, but it just wasn't to be at the time. By the next morning, Wes had come up with a logical explanation. The heavy feeling was probably just all of our imaginations and as far as the lights flickering in response to his questions, well that was just a coincidence, but we obviously had some serious electrical problems.

Being concerned with our "electrical problem," Wes replaced the breaker panel a few days later. I once made the comment that ghosts were the perfect guests. They didn't eat, so they didn't cost much. The young Indian never ate at our house, but he did cost us quite a bit with the price of replacing the breaker box.

This ghost stayed with us for several years. He had a friend in Keshia; he was generally found wherever she was, and of course wherever the lights were flickering. To Wes's disappointment, replacing the breaker box hadn't helped with our "electrical problems" after all.

12: THE STAGE

1999–2001

· · · · · · · · · · · · · · · · · · · ·

A measure of talent that not even the stages of Broadway have ever seen belonged to an entity I'll refer to as The Imitator. The Imitator could change from the role of a male to a female and from an adult to a child seemingly without effort. As many performers have the reputation of being temperamental, I guess she was too, in her own way. Her unpredictable behavior manifested itself by her strong desire to cause chaos within the family, and believe me she did it quite well. I must admit, even though I often bore the brunt of her sense of humor, I can't help but smile just thinking of how much fun she must've had at our expense.

One evening I was cooking dinner when Troy came into the kitchen and asked me what I needed. When I told him I hadn't called for him, he gave me a disbelieving look, because we'd had this conversation many times over the past several days. For reasons I hadn't yet understood, everyone in the house seemed to think I had called for them when I hadn't. With a shake of his head, Troy went back to his room only to return about ten minutes later, asking again what I wanted. When I told him for a second time that I hadn't called for him, he folded his arms across his chest and told me to "stop it." He said he was trying to play a video game and if I didn't need anything, I should quit calling for him.

I think it's safe to say that at one time or another, most people have mistakenly thought someone called for them when in fact no one did. But when the majority of conversations in the household start with, "What did you need?" or "Did you call for me?" one can't help but wonder …

It was getting frustrating for all of us, but it hadn't been a major issue until one day when Keshia and I were in my bedroom talking and we heard Wes run through the house screaming out my name. Keshia and I both jumped at the panic we heard in his voice. Just as I was on my way to the door, Wes threw it open, almost hitting me in the process. His eyes were wild with fear as he asked me what was wrong.

I managed to stammer out that nothing was wrong. With my heart racing, I asked him why he thought there was.

His eyes darted from me to Keshia and, seeing that we were okay, he asked why I had called for him in that "terrified" voice.

When Keshia and I both told him that I hadn't called for him, his panic turned to anger. Holding the towel around his waist with one hand, he jabbed at the air with his other as he said he knew what he had heard. He told us he'd just gotten out of the shower when he heard me scream out his name as though something was terribly wrong. He proceeded to tell us how he could have broken his neck running through the house with wet feet as he tried to find me.

I knew he must have heard someone scream for him, but Keshia and I both knew it wasn't me. As these incidents piled up, Keshia and I came to the conclusion that we had a ghost that could imitate my voice to perfection. Wes and Troy concluded I was just "messing" with them.

Having an entity that could imitate me was a little unnerving, but it didn't stop there. Apparently, she was able to look like me, too—and that was a little bizarre even for our house.

This isn't something I ever dreamed was possible, so when I started hearing comments such as, "How did you get in here so fast? I just saw you in the kitchen," I didn't think anything about it. But when Troy complained about me coming into his room during the night to check on him, I knew something wasn't right. By this time, Troy was twelve or thirteen years old and I hadn't been in his room to "check on him" in years, but according to him, I did it all the time. He said I'd come in his room and cover him up, and when he asked me what I was doing I would tell him I was just checking and for him to go back to sleep.

I was blown away by this. I knew I hadn't been in Troy's room, but apparently, someone who looked and sounded like me had. Between this and everyone always thinking I was calling for them, I was starting to feel a little picked on by this entity. But everyone else was soon to get their turn.

Like any other performer, the longer The Imitator practiced her craft, the better she became. It wasn't long before she was imitating each of our voices. As far as I know, she never physically appeared as anyone other than me, but she could sure sound like them. At times, it seemed as though we'd all lost our minds as we ran around the house saying, "What?"

"What do you mean, 'what'?"

"Did you call me?"

"I didn't call you, I thought you were calling me."

After experiencing this for about three years, we became accustomed to this game. When we heard someone call for us, we'd just yell back "Are you calling for me?" If we didn't get a reply, Keshia and I knew The Imitator was at it again. Since I had given up trying to figure out Wes and Troy's logic on these matters, I wasn't sure how this made any type of sense in their minds, but somehow it did. Their usual response was "I must be hearing things."

When I heard the ghost imitate one of us, I was usually more fascinated than anything, but when she used the voice of someone who wasn't home, that proved to be a little more eerie.

The most common theory about ghosts is, of course, that they are simply the spirits of dead people. Whether this is true or not, that thought was often in my mind and hearing the voice of Wes or one of the children when I knew they weren't home would sometimes cause me to wonder if something had happened to them.

I can remember one time in particular that this thought bothered me all day. Troy had gotten into the habit of making a loud popping sound with his mouth. He knew this irritated me beyond reason, so naturally he did it all the time. One of his favorite things to do was to sneak up behind me and loudly pop into my ear.

After getting the kids off to school, I was standing at the sink washing dishes when I heard the familiar popping sound in my ear. Out of habit, I yelled out Troy's name and told him to quit. When my outburst didn't receive a response, it occurred to me that he was at school. As the silence hung in the air, I had a terrible feeling something might have happened to him. I knew if it were truly possible for the dead to come back, this would be how he would choose to do it.

I continued to hear the popping sound throughout the day. With each pop, my unease grew. Every time the phone rang, I was afraid someone was calling to tell me something had happened to Troy. By the time the school day ended, I was a nervous wreck. When he walked in the door, I was so relieved to see him that when he did his signature pop, he didn't even get into trouble.

Keshia and I admired the abilities The Imitator possessed, no matter how irritating it was at times. But we never had a full understanding of the depth of her talent until she chose to reveal it one day to Keshia while the rest of us had gone to town. Keshia was in her room studying when she heard her dad call out for her. Thinking we had gotten home, she walked into the living room to see what he wanted. Not seeing anyone in the house, she looked out the window and saw our car wasn't home.

She returned to her room. Getting back to her homework, she heard me call for her. Knowing it was probably The Imitator, but not wanting to get into trouble, she again left her room to see if we were home. We weren't. Stomping back to her room, she heard Troy call her from the other end of the house. Frustrated with this game, Keshia called out to The Imitator to quit messing with her. She said she had work to do and she wasn't falling for it anymore.

After working on her homework for about thirty minutes, she heard Wes, Troy, and me in the living room talking. She said she couldn't make out what we were saying, but could distinctly hear each of our voices with the rise and fall of our tones as if we were having a normal, every-day conversation. When she walked into the living room to see how our trip to town had gone, she was greeted with an empty house.

This incredible incident was to be The Imitator's final performance for us. I guess our home proved not to be a big enough stage to fulfill her mischievous desires. The Imitator left us after about three years. Maybe the bright lights of Broadway were calling to her, but wherever she is, I'm certain she's having loads of fun and leaving a lot of confusion in her wake.

13: HIDE AND SEEK

2000–2004

....

Over the years, I've come to realize our home is different from other haunted houses. With information concerning true hauntings being more prevalent now, I've learned that many of these haunted homes are believed to be inhabited by the spirits of former owners. I think that was probably the case with our house and the green glowing ball, but for us, it didn't stop there. After the green ghost left, our house had paranormal activity from so many different entities I came to feel that not only was our home haunted, but possibly our land was too.

Most of these visitors were like the green ghost. They were subtle, doing nothing other than opening and closing a door or just simply allowing us to feel their presence. As with the green ghost, this type of activity could be ignored. The other guests were more obvious, and when we had more than one of these living with us at the same time, things could get interesting. During the time when The Imitator had us all running around like crazy people, we also had a male entity that liked to keep us on our toes. He invented a game of ghostly hide-and-seek. Ghostly being the key word because, without the ability to go through walls, we didn't have a chance of winning this game.

Considering how I like everything to be put in its proper place, this game often pushed me to my limits. For instance, I'd put my purse where it belonged, which was hanging on the back of my chair, but when I went to get it, many times it wouldn't be there. I'd sometimes find it in another room, or even more frustrating, I'd find it a little later hanging on the back of my chair where it should have been earlier, but wasn't.

This game wasn't reserved for me alone; we all experienced it. The kids would lose books, games, uniforms, etc., only to find them in the center of their beds after school. One of the most common items to come up missing was my hairbrush. I kept it in the vanity drawer in my bedroom, but often found it on the dining room table. Considering my obsession with cleanliness, the last place

I would put my brush would be on the table where we ate our meals. Even though this game was an irritant, it wasn't that big of a deal, that is until the day Wes lost an irreplaceable item—his cap.

Like most cap wearers, he had his favorite and it was gone. Finding this cap became his only mission and when he didn't have any luck himself, he made locating it a priority for us all. After all, a cap couldn't just vanish, but from all appearances, it did. We searched the house, the shop, and the vehicles. Running out of places to look, he resigned himself to wearing one of his other caps.

I was sure his cap would turn up in one of the places we already looked just as our other "lost" items had, but it didn't. The cap was gone and eventually left our thoughts, until we found it a year or so later in the most unlikely place.

We were having problems with our whirlpool tub and, to get to the workings of the tub, Wes had to remove the access panel. First, he had to take off the decorative trim, cut the caulking, and then unscrew the solid wood front. Struggling to lift the panel, he abruptly stopped. Looking under the tub, he asked how these things had gotten back there.

Peering over his shoulder, I saw not only his cap, but also a bottle of glue, pencils, bookmarks, tools, and a rag. To me there was only one explanation as to how these items could get behind the solid panel. What I didn't know was how Wes was going to explain it away. I could only hope his explanation wouldn't be as expensive as replacing the electric panel had been.

Even though the ghost clearly cheated, he was good at this game of hide-and-seek. If he didn't want you to find the hidden item, you wouldn't.

Once, Keshia couldn't find the blow-dryer anywhere. She always kept it in the same drawer in her room. After looking in all of her drawers, then under the bed, and in the closet, she asked to borrow mine.

After a few days of using mine, I insisted she call her friends to make certain she hadn't left it at one of their houses. None of her friends had seen it, so I helped her look for it again. Having no luck, we continued to share mine.

After the blow-dryer was missing for three months or so, we realized she was going to need a replacement to take to camp with her. We both looked one final time before I said I'd get her one the next time I went to town. Before I had the chance to go shopping, Keshia came into my room with her blow-dryer, asking me where I'd found it. When I told her I hadn't found it, she told me it was in her drawer where she used to always keep it—the same drawer we'd both looked for it many times. As we laughed, we knew we'd lost another game of hide-and-seek.

14: GHOST HUNTING 101

2004

....

In the summer of 2004, we wanted to go somewhere different for our family vacation. We decided on Eureka Springs, Arkansas. This booming little town survived on tourism and seemed to offer a wide variety of things to do.

In Eureka, we hit all of the family "hot spots" as we filled our days with hiking, shopping, and sightseeing. Almost everywhere we went had a display of brochures of more things to do. One brochure in particular stood out to me. It advertised ghost tours. Typically, convincing Wes and Troy to go on something like this would've been next to impossible. However, this tour went through the famed Crescent Hotel, built in 1886. Wes was a fan of old architecture, so he agreed to go even though that meant having to "suffer" through the tour.

On our way to the hotel, we drove up a steep and winding road with breathtaking scenery. Reaching the top of West Mountain, we saw the Crescent Hotel. I was in awe! Now I understood why the hotel was so popular and why it was referred to as The Grand Old Lady of the Ozarks.

Walking into the hotel, I got a little nervous. None of us had ever been on a ghost tour before and I wasn't sure what to expect. I hoped it wasn't going to be like a fun house Halloween tour with "ghosts" jumping out from around corners and chasing us down the hall. Living with ghosts had made me uncomfortable with those who made a mockery of their existence.

Clairvoyants Carroll Heath and Ken Fugate own and operate The Eureka Springs Ghost Tours. At the time, they were the ones who ran these tours at the Crescent. On this particular night, Carroll was leading the tour and he told the group that we should try to take pictures because many people reported capturing ghostly images on film while taking the tour. He suggested using a digital camera, but said that any camera would work. I'd never tried to take a picture of a ghost before, but I had my 35 mm and was anxious to try.

Soon after the tour started, I saw that my earlier concerns about the tour had been pointless. Carroll led the tour with such integrity and respect that not even Wes or

Troy could find room to complain. The tour consisted of the rich history about the hotel and, of course, we heard the stories about the ghosts that allegedly roamed the halls.

We learned that over the years the hotel had served as many different businesses, and it seemed as though each had left its mark. Almost assuredly, the deepest mark left on the hotel occurred from 1937-1940. During this time, the Crescent Hotel served as a "cancer hospital."

A man by the name of Norman Baker bought the hotel and transformed it into the Baker Hospital and Health Resort. Baker claimed to be able to cure cancer without the use of surgery, radium, or X-ray. The problem was Norman Baker didn't have one day of medical training. His "cancer cure" consisted of a mix of watermelon seed, brown corn silk, alcohol, and carbolic acid. Some believe that many of the ghosts from the Crescent Hotel are former patients of "Dr." Baker.

Hearing the ghost stories and seeing the reactions of the other tour goers helped me realize just how much things had changed over the years. When Wes and I had bought our house twenty years earlier, I couldn't find any information that dealt with ghosts. Now it seemed as though people were much more open to the possibility of their existence and I had a stronger desire than ever to learn more about them—and that was exactly what I planned to do.

The first thing on my agenda was to learn about capturing ghostly images on film as Carroll had talked about.

I was intrigued with this possibility, so as soon as we got home from our vacation, I sent my rolls of film off to be developed. I was surprised to find that, like me, Wes was anxious to get our ghost tour pictures back. For the first time since the encounter with the young Indian ghost, he was showing some interest in the subject.

When I got the pictures back, I flipped through them to find the ones I had taken during the tour. My initial response was one of disappointment. I'm not sure what I was expecting, maybe an apparition holding up a sign that said, "Yes, I'm a ghost." Since that hadn't happened, I took a closer look at the pictures and I noticed many of them contained orbs.

Because of the now-popular ghost-hunting shows, I knew some things about these orbs and Carroll had told us that he, like many others, felt they were the energy of ghosts. Noticing that quite a few of my pictures had orbs, I was a little more impressed. I decided to try to find out more about these orbs.

After doing some research, I found there were two prevailing thoughts. One, orbs are proof of paranormal activity. Two, they are no more than dust particles, raindrops, or bugs. I knew it wasn't raining inside the hotel, so as far as these pictures were concerned, I could check that one off. As for the dust particles and bugs, I just wasn't sure. I hadn't seen any bugs, and the hotel appeared to be too clean for there to have been that much dust floating around. I decided to try a little experiment on my own.

I purchased a digital camera and took it outside. Every time I saw a flying bug, I'd take a picture. None of these pictures resembled an orb. They were either missing the bug altogether or they looked like ... well ... bugs.

Now, on to the dust particles, I took a rug from the hall into the bathroom, and shook it. I snapped a few pictures and I got very similar-looking orbs in these pictures.

After my experiment, I still didn't know what to think of orbs. While reading different opinions about them, I ran across an article that claimed dust particles and paranormal orbs differ in appearance. Some believe dust particles have a dark ring around them while the orbs caused by the energy of an entity do not. I put the pictures—the one from the Crescent Hotel and the one taken in my bathroom—on my computer and enlarged them. All of the known dust orbs had rings around them. The orbs from the Crescent were about half-and-half with some having rings while the others didn't.

Still not sure how I felt about orbs, but now knowing that it was possible to capture ghostly images on film, I kept my camera close by in hopes of capturing something paranormal in my own home. The next time I experienced the familiar sensation of a ghost coming into the room, I was ready. I picked up my camera and announced, "If there's anyone in here, please sit in this chair and let me take your picture." I took several pictures of the chair. Each picture, except for one, showed only the image of the chair.

The picture may have been coincidental, but looking at the chair there was a bright orb that appeared to be in motion and seemed to be emitting its own light. Even after enlarging it by 400%, I couldn't see a ring around it (if you would like to see this photo, it can be found at http://authorlisarogers.weebly.com under the Haunting Images tab).

It seemed as though the more I tried to find out about orbs, the more confused I became. What I did know was that an orb can be produced on film with dust, and an orb can be produced on film by taking a picture outside while it's raining. These are facts I was able to prove to myself, but I still didn't know if an orb ever signified the presence of a ghost.

15: DINNER DEBATE

2004

....

Several family discussions were prompted by my decision to learn more about ghosts. Sharing my thoughts on what orbs might or might not be at the dinner table one night, Wes and Troy fell into their usual skeptical roles. Neither one of them had thought much of the orb photos I'd taken during the ghost tour and when I told them what I'd learned about orbs, they of course went with the idea that the pictures had to be of dust or bugs, because ghosts simply didn't exist.

With that can of worms not only opened, but dumped right on the table, we rehashed the accounts of the green glowing ball, the pictures, the plaques, the missing items, the doors opening and closing, etc. As we continued talking, I realized just how much activity our house had had over the years, and to my surprise, much of it was unknown to Wes and Troy. Since Keshia and I knew how they felt about the subject, we discussed a lot of the activity between ourselves.

Keshia decided to fill them in on some of the activity they didn't know about. First, she recounted a time that she and I were the only ones at home. She had gone to her room in hopes of taking a nap. As she lay in bed with her head partially covered, she heard someone come in. Thinking I wanted her to get up and do something, she quickly closed her eyes and pretended to be asleep. After a minute or two, she peeked out from the covers and, seeing a pair of black-socked feet pass in front of her bed, she assumed her plan had worked and she snuggled back down and went to sleep.

After getting up from her nap, she came into the living room and saw my white-socked feet propped up on the coffee table. Ready to confess that she hadn't really been asleep when I'd come into her room, she asked me why I'd changed my socks. Since I hadn't changed my socks, we concluded one of our ghosts must have been in her room.

When Wes heard the story, he laughed and said that was our problem—anytime something seemed a little unusual, we just automatically assumed it was a ghost. In all probability the sunshine coming in through the window must have cast a shadow on the floor, making my socks appear darker than they were. That actually almost made sense except for the fact that I hadn't gone into Keshia's room at all.

He decided we were either "messing" with him, or that I'd simply forgotten about going in there.

Refusing to be deterred, Keshia said she'd like to see what kind of explanation he could come up with concerning her touch lamp.

In good humor, Wes readjusted his ball cap and told her he had his sleuthing cap ready and for her to bring on the next mystery and he'd solve it too.

After making sure that he remembered the touch lamp we'd gotten her for one of her birthdays, she told him that it would turn itself on in the middle of the night and wake her up.

Wes put his hand up, halting the conversation. He told her she'd have to do better than that to challenge him. He said that this mystery was the easiest one yet to explain away. With a smug grin, he pronounced that the lamp must have had a short in it.

Matching his self-righteous attitude, Keshia shook her head and told him that he hadn't let her finish telling the story. She continued by saying she had thought of that too, and that is why she unplugged the lamp and wrapped the cord around its base. With a little smugness of her own, she told him she wanted to know how, even after she had unplugged it, that it continued to turn itself on in the middle of the night.

Wes rubbed his forehead as he told her that was an impossibility and it couldn't have happened that way—period.

Keshia simply replied there were a lot of things that went on in our home that should be impossible, but they happened quite frequently and the only way to make any sense of it was to believe in ghosts.

At that point, Wes teasingly slapped his hands on the table and bellowed out, "If there are any ghosts in here they're going to have to prove it to me. Give me a sign! Do something to let me know you're here."

On cue, a picture hanging on the wall rose above the knickknacks on the shelf below, and then fell to the floor. Shocked, we all sat in stunned silence. Wes regained his composure and said something about that being pretty cool, even if it was a coincidence.

The picture coming off the wall shocked me, but not as much as his blatant denial. Even Troy told Wes that he was on his own this time.

Wes got up from the table and picked up the picture. Inspecting it, he said, "Oh, come on, it was a coincidence. It had to be!" After hanging it back up, he pointed out the fact that the knickknacks on the shelf below the picture stood higher than the bottom of the frame. He commented on how the knickknacks should have fallen to the floor.

Still amazed at his stubbornness, I told him the picture hadn't fallen, that it was purposely taken off the wall.

16: EVPs

2005

....

With ghost-hunting shows now being so popular, I saw that some groups were trying to prove the existence of ghosts through scientific means. One way they were doing this was using digital voice recorders to try to capture a disembodied voice. The thought is that the frequencies of these voices are sometimes well below the range of sounds that are audible to the human ear. When one of these voices is recorded, it is referred to as an EVP (electronic voice phenomena).

Even though EVPs have recently gotten more attention, this isn't a new concept. In the 1920s, Thomas

Edison told a reporter from *Scientific American* magazine that he was working on a machine that would have the ability to contact the dead. He wasn't able to complete this task before his own death, but he did believe it would one day be possible to record the voice of a ghost.

After learning all I could about EVPs, I bought a digital voice recorder. The model I purchased came with a voice activation mode, which meant you could set it to record only if there was a noise.

So I set the recorder on this mode and quietly left it in a room by itself. I'd heard it took a lot of patience to capture an EVP, so when I went to check on it a little later I was surprised to see that it had already recorded something.

Willing my trembling fingers to work, I pushed the playback button. With the recorder pressed tightly to my ear, I held my breath and listened. I strained to make sense of the odd guttural noises coming through the speaker. Then I recognized the sound. The recorder had picked up our dogs barking outside. Period. No disembodied voice—just dogs.

I was so disappointed, but also determined not to give up. The next day I tried again. That time I captured the sounds of birds singing. This was going to be harder than I thought, but I kept trying, and trying, and trying. I had gotten in the routine of turning the recorder on two or three times a week. Sometimes I left the recorder in different rooms of the house and at other times, I sat down beside it and asked questions, but still had no luck.

In the process of dyeing my hair one day, I decided to get the recorder out and try again. After setting it in the hallway, I went to another part of the house and waited until it was time to rinse my hair. On my way to the shower, I picked up the recorder and saw it had recorded something. Being used to this by now, I didn't get too excited. I knew it had probably recorded the icemaker, or crickets, or some other explainable noise. I pushed the playback button. As the recorder started to play, I was prepared to hit the delete button as was routine. But this time, I heard a voice. It was a raspy, whispering male voice say what I thought was, "I'm coming, I'm coming up."

This was what I'd hoped for. This was what I'd tried for weeks to accomplish, but upon hearing the voice, instead of being excited, I was pretty much terrified. I promptly threw the recorder down the hallway. As it laid spinning on the floor, my mind screamed. *I have to get out of here! I have to leave—now!*

If not for my vanity, I'm sure I would've run from the house. Before I made it to the front door, I realized if I didn't at least rinse the dye from my hair it would burn beyond recognition, and that somehow gave me the courage I needed to stay. I told myself I'd take a quick shower and then leave.

As I fumbled around in the shower, my senses slowly returned and excitement replaced my fear. After all, I now had undisputable proof. By the time I got out of the shower, I calmed down enough to want to hear the recording again, and again, and again. I couldn't wait for Wes to get home. After all these years, I was going to be able to prove to him that ghosts did exist.

As it turns out, my recording proved nothing to anyone. Neither Wes, nor either one of the kids, could make anything out of the recording. They were indifferent. They told me they *thought* they could hear a voice, but they couldn't be sure.

It took all the restraint I had not to scream. To me it was so plain. I couldn't understand why no one else could hear it. When Troy suggested that I could hear it only because I wanted too, I told them I was simply giving up.

Of course my giving up was only temporary. Soon, I was back into the routine of trying to get another EVP. Within just a few days, I took my recorder back into the hall where I had recorded the previous voice and I tried again. This time I sat down and turned the recorder on. At first, I was being very quiet and trying not to make any noise at all. Then I asked, "Is anyone here?" After waiting for a response, I continued, "What is your name?" After ten or fifteen minutes, I decided to end the recording session for the day.

I pushed the playback button and listened. I heard the sound of footsteps. This was strange. I'd been sitting down the whole time, so I knew the footsteps weren't mine and I hadn't heard them while I was sitting there. Next, I heard what sounded like someone exhaling with their mouth right over the microphone. Then I heard my voice as I asked questions. Right after I asked, "What is your name?" that same raspy male voice said what I thought was, "I'm Paul." A cold chill ran down my spine, but to my credit, I somehow managed to refrain from throwing the recorder this time.

The recording was good, but I tried not to get my hopes up. I had thought the last recording was good, too, and no one else had been nearly as impressed with it as I had been. Regardless, once everyone got home, I brought my recorder into the living room and said I wanted them to listen to something.

Upon hearing the recording, Wes immediately sat up a little straighter in his chair. Looking intently at the recorder, he asked me to play it again.

He'd heard it! I gushed with excitement as I said, "I think when I asked him what his name was he said, 'I'm Paul.'"

Wes shook his head. "I don't think so."

My heart sank. *Of course you don't!*

Wes cleared his throat and, in a shaky voice, he told me that he thought the voice had said "Grandpa."

"What?" I stuttered.

Wes was visibly shaken. He whispered, "I think he said 'Grandpa.'"

Both of the kids agreed that the recording sounded as though the voice had said, "Grandpa."

I was ecstatic! They'd all heard the voice. Troy wasn't sure what to make of it and Wes's only comment was that it shook him to his bones.

After this, Wes was much more interested in the possibility of capturing an EVP. One night after the kids had gone to bed, he asked me to get the recorder and show him how I tried to record one of these voices. This was a huge step for him.

I got the recorder, turned it on, and placed it in the doorway. Wes and I sat down and I signaled for him to be quiet. After a short time, I asked, "Is anybody in here?" I waited. "Can you tell me your name?"

I halfway expected Wes to start laughing, but he sat very quietly and listened. He was taking it all very seriously. As we continued to sit there, I felt someone walk up and stand behind my chair. I turned, thinking it was one of the children. Seeing no one, I asked, "Is someone behind me?" The sensation left as if they had walked away.

After a few minutes, I got the recorder and brought it back to where Wes and I were sitting. I pushed the play button. We could hear me ask questions and then a male voice responded. This voice was different from the ones I'd captured before. Even though the voice was clear, we couldn't make out what it said. It sounded like he was speaking a different language.

Wes slumped back in his chair as he told me that this was simply impossible. Looking around the room he asked, "Where did that voice come from?"

Being a firm believer in ghosts, I could still relate to Wes's reaction. There is something a little creepy about recording one of these voices. As we both sat trying to make sense of it, I wondered if the recording could be the voice of the young Indian. I didn't know if he was still here, but I knew he had been as recently as a year ago.

I knew because one evening after Keshia had gone to bed, I remembered something I needed to tell her. I went into her room and saw her lying on her back with both arms under the covers and down at her sides, and the blankets all neatly tucked in around her. I asked how she'd managed to tuck herself in like that.

She told me she wasn't the one who had done it. She went on to explain that the Indian ghost generally tucked her in. She calmly explained that when she got into bed at night, he would pat her cheek, tuck her in, and sit on the far corner of her bed until she went to sleep.

I shuddered as I noticed the depression in the blankets at the foot of her bed. I hadn't thought about the young Indian ghost in years and I had no idea he was still around. I'd always prided myself on just being able to accept the fact that we had ghosts, but I must say Keshia probably slept much more soundly than I did that night.

17: THE TREE BENDS

2005–2006

. . . .

Whether it was the picture coming off the wall when Wes asked for a sign or our recent luck with the EVP recordings, the tide was changing. Wes and Troy were both having some doubts concerning their skepticism in ghosts. Wes would now admit there was something unusual going on in our home, but it wasn't a ghost and no further explanation seemed required. Troy, at least, gave the "something" a name: the wind. Even indoors, with all windows and doors closed, if something happened, "it was the wind." The wind in our home turned off lights, moved objects, and mimicked voices. To this day, I have no idea where

Troy's explanation of "the wind" came from, but, for him, it made more sense than living in a haunted house.

The problem, I'd learned, of blaming the strange activity at our home on a ghost stemmed from our religious beliefs. Like many other Christians, Wes and Troy felt as though believing in ghosts somehow couldn't coincide with their belief in God. Keshia and I had no problem with believing in both. The Bible spoke of ghosts. Matthew 14:26 states, "And when the disciples saw Him walking on the sea, they were frightened, saying, 'It is a ghost!' And they cried out for fear."

Keshia and I drew from that passage that ghosts indeed existed. Anyone who is familiar with the Bible knows that Jesus was a great teacher and He used every opportunity He had to educate. Keshia and I felt if ghosts weren't real, Jesus would've used this time to teach that fact to his disciples. However, He didn't deny the existence of ghosts, but instead, in the following verse He said, "Take courage, it is I; do not be afraid." I think it's important to note He didn't tell His disciples ghosts didn't exist. He just said, "It is I."

To Wes and Troy, just because Jesus didn't deny ghosts' existence in this passage didn't necessarily mean that He confirmed their existence either, so the debate continued. One day Wes came to me with a Bible passage he'd found. Handing me his Bible, he asked me to read Luke 24: 37-39. I began aloud, "But they were startled and frightened and thought that they were seeing a spirit. And He said to them, 'Why are you troubled, and why do doubts arise in your hearts? See My hands and My feet, that it is I Myself; touch Me and see, for a spirit does not have flesh and bones as you see that I have.'"

Wes asked me to read the last part again.

I read aloud, "For a spirit does not have flesh and bones as you see that I have."

Taking his Bible, he slowly reread the passage. He then asked if I thought Jesus was confirming the existence of ghosts, or spirits, when He said they don't have flesh and bones.

I had never really thought about this passage before, but the way it read did make it seem like a confirmation of their existence. I was thrilled to see Wes using his Bible to study this topic. After twenty-one years of marriage, I viewed his stance on ghosts as unbendable. I thought no matter what he witnessed he would never change his mind, but his attitude was shifting.

It was almost too much to hope for, but it seemed as though he was really starting to see things differently. He was more inquisitive about the activity that went on in our home and he frequently asked questions. He still wasn't "buying into it all," but he was at least thinking about the possibilities.

I didn't realize how much his mind-set had changed until he agreed to take me to a ghost-hunting seminar that I'd asked to go to for my birthday. Staring at the tickets in my hand, I still couldn't believe it. I was going to get to go ... to the seminar ... to the *ghost* seminar with ... *Wes.*

The seminar was going to be conducted at the Crescent Hotel by the Eureka Springs Ghost Tour Company. It was to include four days and three nights' stay. During this time, each of the guests would participate in an investigation of the hotel. This meant we'd be going into areas that were typically not accessible to visitors. The seminar also included classes taught by clairvoyants Carroll Heath and Ken Fugate, the owners of the Eureka Springs Ghost Tour Company.

After the shock of getting to go started to wear off, reality set in and I started getting concerned of how Wes was going to handle four days of being around "a bunch of crazy people." He'd become more interested in the subject of ghosts, but this I wasn't so sure about. He still claimed to be a skeptic, so I expressed my concerns and asked him if he would try to keep an open mind while we were at the seminar.

His reply of, "I've told you before, if you have too open of a mind then all of your sense falls out," did little to ease my fears.

As my apprehension grew, he finally told me I had nothing to worry about. He acknowledged that this wasn't something he'd typically agree to do. But, considering the things that went on in our house, he was curious to find out a little more.

With his assurance and my renewed excitement, we arrived at the Crescent Hotel on January 12, 2006. Our first class was to meet in the Governor's Suite at the hotel for refreshments and a meet-and-greet session.

The directors, Ken and Carroll, asked each of the participants to start by introducing themselves and tell what had prompted them to come to the seminar. When it was my turn, I introduced Wes and myself to the group. I told them I'd always believed in ghosts, whereas Wes, for the most part, didn't. I explained that our house was haunted and being on opposite sides of this issue had created some minor problems for us over the years.

Upon hearing that we lived in a haunted house, the other guests were interested to know what types of activity we'd experienced in our home. I told about some of the recent activity including the picture coming off the wall when Wes had asked for a sign. When I relayed his response of "It was a coincidence," the room exploded with laughter.

Being the only skeptic in the room Wes knew he was in for a little harassment, and the group didn't disappoint. He took the teasing in the manner it was given and was good-natured about it. This time he was the oddball and I have to admit, in a sick and twisted sort of way, I kind of liked it.

After joining in on the fun and taking his turn at picking on Wes, Ken decided it was break time. As I went out on the porch for coffee, I saw that Wes was surrounded by the other guests. As I walked up to the group, I heard one of the women ask him how it was possible for him not to believe after seeing the picture come off the wall.

He smiled and shrugged as he told her that there could have been a logical explanation.

She continued to tease him for a little while as she told him she thought he was running out of excuses. She asked him what was so hard about admitting that we had a ghost.

He told her he had a logical mind and that ghosts just didn't fit into his box.

She laughed. "Logical mind, phhhf!" She patted him on the back and told him he obviously needed a bigger box.

The next morning, when the classes started, Carroll began by talking about energy. He explained that we're all made up of energy and we all have our own energy field, or aura, around us. Carroll sat down in the middle of the floor. He said he wanted each of us to take turns coming up to him to try to feel the energy field around him. This was all new to me. Taking my turn, I was surprised that I really could feel this energy.

After everyone had their turn of trying to feel Carroll's energy, Ken asked Wes if he could try something with him. He asked Wes to stand up, close his eyes, and hold one of his hands, palm out, in front of him. Ken went to the far side of the room, put his hand up, and made the motion as if he were pushing on Wes's hand. He told Wes to let him know if he felt anything.

With his eyes closed, Wes told him that he could feel him pushing on his hand.

Ken told him to keep his hand out in front of him, but to open his eyes. When Wes opened his eyes and saw that Ken was eight or more feet from him, he wasn't sure what to think.

Ken told him to keep his hands up as he moved four or five feet further away. He began tapping the air with his index finger. After a few taps he asked Wes if he could feel it.

Wes dropped his hand. "That's freaky!" He sat down and asked Ken how that was possible.

Taking a seat himself, Ken explained that Wes was simply feeling his energy. He told Wes that, with his co-operation, he was going to learn a lot during the seminar that he never thought was possible.

I was intrigued! I knew Wes had felt Ken touch him from across the room. Like Wes, I didn't understand how Ken had achieved it, but I wanted to know more. Even though I found this topic fascinating, I didn't understand what any of this had to do with ghosts until Ken explained that it was possible to feel the energy from a ghost in the same manner. He then told us we were going to do a meditation exercise to help us become more sensitive to this energy.

Meditation? Oh boy, isn't that when people sit on a mountaintop and chant with flowers in their hair? What have I gotten us into?

Ken told us to sit up straight in our chairs with our feet planted firmly on the floor. Desperately trying to think of a tactful way out of this, I heard him tell everyone to close their eyes and take a deep breath.

Not knowing what else to do, I closed my eyes. I had never tried to meditate before and I wasn't sure what to expect. As Ken's soothing voice guided the group, I peeked over at Wes to see how he was handling this new experience. I was surprised to see that, unlike me, he was doing what was asked of him.

Taking Wes's lead, I began following the instructions, too. It was very different from what I'd expected. When the meditation ended, I felt as though I had just taken a much-needed nap. I was rejuvenated and ready to learn.

Pairing up into teams, the group was ready to practice feeling for energy again. The meditation helped to improve my sensitivity. With Wes as my partner, I was able to locate the perimeter of his energy field without any difficulty.

Even though Wes and I could both detect the energy, we discovered that we experienced a different sensation when we touched it. Wes said that to him it felt as though someone was blowing on his hand. With me, I felt as though I was pressing my hands against a tightly filled balloon.

When Ken and Carroll were satisfied with everyone's progress, they said it was time to put what we'd learned to use. It was time for us to start the investigation of the hotel.

18: THE INVESTIGATION

2006

....

The opportunity to investigate the Crescent Hotel with Ken and Carroll was like a dream come true. Sitting in their classes for a day and a half, I had already learned so much and I was ready to put my new knowledge to work.

Our group was excited to find that our first investigation of the hotel was to start in the basement. This area is very large and is divided between public and private use. The public area contains restrooms, a lobby, and a spa. The private area, only used by the hotel staff, contains the laundry room, storage, and various workrooms. When the hotel served as Dr. Baker's Cancer Hospital, this was where the morgue was located and to this day, still holds the autopsy table.

At 10:00 p.m., we went down the stairs and stopped in front of the spa. With the business closed for the night, Ken told everyone to make themselves comfortable on the stairs or in the lobby. As he started to go over our itinerary for the evening, he abruptly quit talking.

After a few seconds of silence, Ken asked if anyone could feel anything. I was surprised to hear Wes say that he could. With my attention now focused on him, I could see that he looked a little uneasy. When Ken asked Wes to describe what he felt, I started taking pictures.

Wes said he felt a cold spot on the back of his hand. He lifted his hands and vigorously rubbed one with the other. He visibly shuddered as he told the group that it felt like someone had laid a block of ice on his hand.

With everyone's attention turned to Wes, Ken pointed out that Wes's hands had been hanging down to his sides. He said that was an interesting point because Wes's hands were down low and a little boy by the name of Christopher had just walked up beside him. Ken said that the boy knew why we were there and he wanted to help us all understand. Even though I couldn't see anything out of the ordinary, I continued taking pictures.

After a few minutes, Ken nodded his head as if he were having a conversation with someone the rest of us couldn't see. He smiled and said "Thank you" to the invisible Christopher. He then told us Christopher had run up the stairs. I aimed my camera towards the staircase and took more pictures. Glancing at the screen on my digital camera, I saw that I'd photographed an orb. *Hmm, that's interesting.* Mentally marking this picture as one I wanted to look at better on the computer, I heard Ken say that it wasn't uncommon to find Christopher in this area of the hotel. He said Christopher always appeared to him as a child, but that didn't necessarily mean he'd died as a child. Ken explained that spirits could choose to come back at any age and that many times they chose to come back as children because that's when they were at their happiest.

As Ken went on to describe, in detail, what Christopher was wearing, I just didn't know what to think. This was weird, even for my standards. I'd always considered myself sensitive to the presence of ghosts and I hadn't seen or felt anything. If Ken hadn't already made such an impression on me during our classes, I would have probably discounted everything he said about the little boy. However, the main thing I'd learned from Ken and Carroll was that I still had a lot to learn.

Bringing me out of my thoughts, I heard Ken unlock the door to the private area of the basement—the area that once was the morgue. As we walked down the hall, Ken told us that most of the downstairs area was a known hot spot for ghostly activity. Ken and Carroll suggested we practice what we'd learned and try to feel for areas that contained unexplainable fields of energy.

With my thoughts still focused on "the little boy," I stood off to the side and waited on Wes. As I watched the group walk down the hall with their hands out in front of them, I couldn't help but feel as though I was caught up in some bizarre zombie movie. I'd seen people do this on ghost-hunting shows before, but I'd never understood why they did it. Even though I now understood, I still found I was a little self-conscious about doing it myself.

I didn't see Wes and I wondered if he had chosen to sit this exercise out. Continuing to watch the group pass with their hands outstretched in front of them, I decided if Wes were sitting this one out, I would gladly join him. I went in the opposite direction of the group, looking for Wes and my jaw dropped as I saw him coming down the hall with his hands stretched out in front of him.

His willingness to experiment with these exercises really surprised me. I was the one who wanted to come to the seminar and yet he seemed to be a more eager participant than I was. When I fell in behind him, he reminded me not to follow too close behind or I wouldn't be able to tell if I was feeling his energy or the energy from something else.

The "morgue" area divides into several rooms. I looked for the room that had the least number of people. For one, I was still self-conscious about doing this exercise and, as Wes had said, I needed some space to try to do this right. Walking into one of the larger rooms, I noticed there were only two other people in there, one of whom was Carroll. Putting my inhibitions aside, with my hands out in front of me, I walked around.

Walking in front of what had once been the autopsy table, I felt something. I stopped. I had the same sensation on the palms of my hands that I had earlier in class when I'd felt Wes's energy. The difference was, there was no one standing in front of me. As I moved my hands around, I could tell this wall of energy started about two feet off the ground and went up a little higher than my head. I backed away and started again. When I approached the same area, I felt it again.

I turned to see Carroll watching me from a corner. I continued with the exercise. Each time my hand roamed over into that one spot, I experienced that "rubber balloon" feel. I turned to Carroll again. He smiled and nodded as he told me that I had it. Seeing my confusion, he said I was feeling the energy of a man who used to work in the morgue and that he'd encountered him many times in that spot.

At home, I'd had a ghost touch me before, but I'd never tried to touch one of them. This was amazing! After leaving the area for awhile, I returned and tried to locate the energy again. It wasn't there. I backed up and tried again. It still wasn't there. Carroll was still standing in the corner and I looked over at him. He shrugged and told me that the man had left.

Even though the investigation lasted well into the night, after going to our room, we couldn't sleep. As we sat and talked, I asked Wes about his experience with the cold spot on his hand. Not wanting to talk about it, he quickly described the same thing to me as he had to the group earlier.

Always being the one to look for a logical explanation, he was bothered with the fact he couldn't find one. Deep in thought, he rubbed the back of his hand and paced the length of our hotel room a few times. When I tried to bring up his experience with the cold spot again, he told me he needed to clear his head and he suggested we go walk the halls of the hotel.

Roaming the halls, we saw another couple from the seminar. I remembered their names were Don and Susan. As I was about to say hello, Wes greeted them by asking if they really believed in all of this stuff. At that point, my only wish was to melt into the floor.

Susan smiled as she gave him an unwavering yes. Speaking for her and her husband, she said they tried to be very open-minded. I was hoping against all hope Wes wouldn't say something about their brains falling out. Luckily, Don stepped into the conversation by asking us if we were the ones who lived in a haunted house.

Hoping to keep Wes quiet, I jumped into the conversation by talking about our ghosts.

Finding out Don and Susan also suspected their home might be haunted, our talk turned to EVPs. After sharing our recordings with them, we realized we had been standing in the hall for over an hour. With our next scheduled class only a few hours away, we said our good-byes and went to our rooms.

Openly talking about ghosts with someone outside of the family had been a unique and enjoyable experience for me. It was comforting to know that other "normal" people experienced some of the same things I had. The conversation seemed to have had the opposite effect on Wes. Combining his experience with the cold spot and meeting another couple who believed in ghosts had his brain on overload. Little did he know, his brain was going to have to do a bit more expanding.

19: CHRISTOPHER'S SECRET

2006

....

The last day of the seminar ended too soon. Attending more classes on meditation and getting to investigate the "most haunted" rooms at the hotel made me want to learn even more. Going to bed that night, I couldn't believe the seminar was already over. The last three days had been wonderful and it was nice to see Wes take an interest in something that was so important to me.

Even though we had already talked about coming back, before we packed to go home, I wanted to go out to the balcony one more time, walk the gardens one more time, and of course, roam the halls and take pictures one more time. Wes was cooperative with all of my wishes, but he was unusually quiet.

Pulling out of the parking lot, I admired the beauty of the Ozarks while he appeared to be deep in thought. Finally breaking the silence, I asked him if he'd had a good time.

"Uh huh," was his only reply.

We continued to drive through the mountains in silence. After an hour of hearing nothing but the roar of the engine, I asked him if something was wrong.

He took a while to answer and when he finally did, he told me he was just trying to get his mind around everything he'd experienced during the seminar. After another ten miles or so he said, "Let me put it this way, all of my life I've been taught that two plus two equals four. Now you and the rest of those people aren't only telling me it equals five, but you're proving it to me."

Proving it to him? Hmmm. After reassuring him that two plus two still equaled four, I asked him if this meant he now believed in ghosts. Wes looked drained as he replied that he didn't know what to believe anymore. Coming to terms with the fact ghosts might exist was causing quite a battle in his head. I knew it was hard on him, but at the same time, I wanted him to draw his own conclusions, so I remained quiet.

As we drove on, he interrupted the silence by telling me he thought he might be losing his mind because he could feel…something at the Crescent. He cleared his throat and asked how "you people" could tell if a ghost was around.

Assuming "you people" referred to those of us who believed in ghosts, I answered the simplest way I knew how. I explained that it felt the same way it does when anyone else walks in the room. Watching the lines of confusion etch his face, I tried to put it another way. "Say you're in a room by yourself, maybe reading or doing something with your head down. If someone walks in, don't you know it before you actually see them?"

When he nodded, I told him I thought we all had that sense, but most people tended to ignore it if their other senses didn't kick in and verify what they thought they felt. The silence resumed.

His face was taut as we barreled down the highway. With his fingers tapping the steering wheel, he told me he wanted to ask me a serious question and he didn't want me to joke around about it. Taking a deep breath, he said, "Do you honestly think we have ghosts in our house?"

He knew what my answer would be, but I said "Yes," for what must have been the hundredth time. His jaw clenched as he continued down the highway.

After getting home, unpacking, and tending to things around the house, I noticed Wes was acting... well... weird. He kept walking from room to room. Normally his walk sounds more like a stomp; it can be heard from all over the house. But not that day. It was almost as if he was sneaking around. He walked quietly, and kept peeking around the corners.

I couldn't help but think that maybe the seminar had been too much for him. *First, two plus two equaled five, and now he's slinking around the house trying to … what? Sneak up on the ghosts?* I finally asked him what he was doing.

At first, he acted as though he'd been caught doing something wrong. As his eyes roamed around the room, he asked me if *they* were here.

When I asked if by *they* he meant the ghosts, he nodded. He looked as though he expected one to jump out at him any minute.

I'd always wanted him to acknowledge that ghosts existed, but now I wasn't so sure. The seminar had … changed him. Almost missing my firmly rooted husband, I told him the ghosts were usually around the house somewhere, but he shouldn't worry about them.

Semi-returning to normal, he told me he wasn't *worried* about them. He just wanted to know if they were around.

The following morning brought the usually dreaded Monday where we all had to return to our normal routines. But I was looking forward to this particular Monday. I was anxious to get everyone out the door so I could put the pictures on the computer and see if I'd captured anything paranormal.

When the front door closed for the final time that morning I grabbed my digital camera and loaded my pictures onto the computer. Looking through the pictures, I came upon the photos I'd taken of Wes when he'd said he felt a cold spot on the back of his hand. Because of the circumstances, I took a little extra time examining them. Some of the pictures had turned out dark, so I lightened them. As I looked, I noticed there was something odd on top of Wes's shoulder in one of the pictures. I couldn't quite make it out so I enlarged the photo. Now something else had my attention! The anomaly on his shoulder was interesting, but looking at the area by Wes's ear made my heart race.

I recalled Ken's words about a little boy named Christopher who had joined the group. Looking at the picture, I could see the silhouette of what appeared to be a little boy whispering in Wes's ear. This was unbelievable! If someone showed me this picture, I would assume it was a fake. It was just too good to be true. But I'd taken this picture and I knew it was real. This had to be the image of Christopher.

I scrutinized each picture again. I had several shots of Wes standing in the same position, and in the same spot, but Christopher only appeared in this one photo (if you would like to see this photo, it can be found at http://authorlisarogers.weebly.com under the Haunting Images tab).

Since Wes was standing in front of a glass door, some have suggested this could be the reflection of a real child, but the picture was taken during a private tour with only adults in attendance.

I couldn't accomplish anything that day. I kept going back to the computer and looking at the picture. It was so unbelievable that now I was the one looking for a logical explanation. I was still looking at the picture when Wes called home on his lunch break. Forgetting that I'd been concerned about his state of mind the night before, I asked him what Christopher had said to him.

After a long pause, he asked me why I would ask him a question like that. Hearing the tension in his voice made me remember his frame of mind. Now wishing I hadn't brought this up on the phone, I tried to be a little more delicate. Using my best motherly voice, I described the picture I was looking at.

Apparently, he hadn't needed to hear my motherly voice because he burst out laughing. He told me I must be seeing things and that there had to be a logical explanation. The old Wes was back.

Sitting at the computer most of the day, I heard Troy come in from school. I jumped up and met him at the door. I *needed* to share this with someone. I took him by the arm and led him to the computer room. I told him I thought I had taken a picture of a ghost.

"Awww, Mom." Troy plopped down in the chair. He looked at the computer screen and asked why I had him looking at a picture of his dad.

My excitement bubbled over as I told him to look closer.

He laughed as he told me all he could see was a picture of his dad.

I couldn't believe this! It was so plain. The memory of my first EVP danced around in my head. Was I really going to be the only one who could see this? I traced the face with my finger on the computer screen. "You don't see the little boy that looks like he's whispering in your dad's ear?"

About that time, Troy's back stiffened. "Wow! I see it!"

"Isn't that awesome?"

"It's something all right." He got up to leave. Seeing my disappointment, he said, "It's cool Mom, but it's just not my thing."

Wes was the next one to come home. Walking in the door, he told me to let him see it. I already had the picture enlarged and on the computer screen. He sat down. "I see something there on my shoulder, but I'm not seeing what you're ... Wait a minute! No, no possible way! This can't be!" Wes shook his head, rubbed his eyes, and turned back to the computer. "This is awesome."

Awesome? You mean no trying to explain it away by some mysterious gasses floating around that happened to form the shape of a child's head as I snapped the photo? Wow, maybe the seminar was worth it after all.

When Keshia came in the house, Wes yelled out, asking her to come to the computer room. He got up to let her have the chair as he told her to look at the picture.

She sat down and studied the photo. With Wes and me peering over her shoulder she knew she was supposed to be seeing something, but she hadn't spotted it yet. Just as I was about to point to the silhouette she said, "Wait a minute! Oh wow!" She leaned back in the chair. "That is cool."

Conversation over the picture consumed the evening. Every few minutes, one of us was back at the computer looking at the picture. We tried to figure out what, if not a ghost, had made that image appear next to Wes's ear.

Wes was handling this much better than I originally thought he would. He wasn't making any excuses, or trying to come up with "logical explanations." He took it for what it was—an amazingly awesome picture. After both of the children went to bed, I asked him again if he was sure that Christopher never said anything to him.

He told me he knew I was going to think he was crazy, but he kept getting an overwhelming feeling of "Everything's going to be okay." He said he never heard a voice, but this thought kept repeating over and over in his head.

I didn't think he was crazy. It made perfect sense. Ken had said Christopher was there to help us understand and he came to Wes, the only skeptic in the group.

2006

....

It took awhile for things to settle down after returning home from the seminar. In all honesty, it took quite awhile. The "box" Wes once proudly kept in order had exploded into tiny little pieces. He added to his own turmoil by insisting Keshia and I tell him every ghost encounter we could recall. Typically, these stories ended with us saying, "No, I'm not kidding," and "I don't know why you didn't believe me."

The seminar had changed Wes so much that after being home for only a few days, Troy came to me and asked what we had done to his dad. He told me he thought

Wes was going off the deep end. Keshia joined in with, "Going?" Her assessment was that he'd already snapped.

Watching Wes jump at every sound as he rocked back and forth in the chair, I began to wonder if maybe the kids were right. His acceptance of ghosts had turned his world upside down. It seemed as though he'd gone from one extreme to the other. In times past, he'd come up with the most absurd explanations to try to explain away any paranormal activity. Now, if the icemaker made a noise or if a dish fell from the drainer, he'd think it was a ghost. I tried to be patient. After all, if he really was going bonkers, I guess I was to blame.

My patience started to diminish when Wes began talking about ghosts to everyone we knew. This left me, at times, wishing he'd turn back just a little bit. I was convinced that people with little white jackets were going to show up on our doorstep and take us all away. This new Wes was going to take some getting used to—a lot of getting used to.

It seemed our entire household was out of balance. As if dealing with Wes wasn't bad enough, Troy felt it his duty to show every person who walked through our door the picture of Christopher. He still didn't admit to believing in ghosts, but he couldn't get enough of showing that picture. Going through the living room one day, I heard a friend of Troy's exclaim, "No way, dude! You're messing with me."

Without seeing what they were doing, I thought Troy had probably gotten Christopher's picture out again. I was so accustomed to keeping my belief in ghosts quiet that all of this newfound openness left me feeling very uncomfortable. I was trying to make my way through the house unnoticed when I heard Troy call to me to come there for a minute. As I walked in, I saw my suspicions were correct. Both boys were huddled around the photo. Troy asked me to tell his friend Bill the picture was "for real."

"Well, okay," I stammered, "it's for real."

Leaning in for a closer look, Bill said, "It's the wind."

The wind, huh? Obviously this wasn't the first time he and Troy had discussed this topic. Putting my discomfort aside, I asked Bill if he believed in ghosts. He told me he wasn't sure, but he didn't think so. He continued by telling me his sister claimed their house was haunted, but he'd never seen any evidence of that. Laying the picture down, he said if anyone's house was haunted it would have to be ours.

Misunderstanding him, I told him I hadn't taken the picture at our house. He said he knew that, but our house was "weird." He went on to tell me he hadn't meant that in a bad way. It was just that crazy things happened here, especially in Troy's room. When I asked him what he was talking about, he shrugged, "Stuff, you know, like things move around and you can hear people walking out in the hall. And that thing with the light was just freaky."

My desire to know what Bill meant dominated my reluctance to talk about ghosts, so I asked him about the light. He said that a year or so before, when he was spending the night, he couldn't go to sleep because of the light shining through the louvers of Troy's closet door. Not finding a switch, he finally woke Troy up and asked him to turn it off so he could get to sleep.

"There is no light in Troy's closet."

Bill said that's why it was "freaky," because there had been a light shining out of it that night.

I'd never heard anything about this, so of course I was intrigued. I asked Troy if he'd actually seen the light as well. When he nodded his confirmation, I asked him why he'd never told me about it before. He laughed. "It was just a light. It wasn't that big of a deal."

Troy's view on these happenings always left me baffled. He didn't deny them or try to come up with explanations, but they didn't seem to warrant much consideration either. It appeared Bill's views were much like Troy's. I asked him what he'd done when he found out Troy didn't have a light in his closet. He said since there wasn't anything he could do about it, he just rolled over and went to sleep.

Life was easier when talk of ghosts was just between Keshia and me. Troy's unbelief/belief just kept me confused, and Wes was … still adjusting. Because of his, shall we say, fragile state of mind, I didn't give it much consideration when he told me he thought the job site he was working on was haunted.

He was working on a major remodel for a large apartment complex. Because the complex was so spread out, he often found himself working alone in the individual apartments. Despite this fact, he complained he kept feeling as though someone was watching him. He also talked about how he'd find his tools in places he knew he hadn't left them.

Thinking my poor husband had gone over the edge, I now found myself trying to come up with logical explanations for the things he was experiencing. When that didn't work, I simply tried to change the subject. I'd always wanted Wes to come to terms with the fact that ghosts existed but this … was just too much.

Trimming apartments, Wes and I had a system. After he got several buildings trimmed out, I'd join him on the job site to install the doorknobs, closet rods, etc. My first day on the job, he kept asking me if I "felt" anything and if I thought the complex was haunted. I hadn't and I didn't. These apartments were no different from the hundreds we'd worked on before. I thought this was just more of his nuttiness.

It took me a couple of weeks to install the hardware and in that time, I hadn't seen anything out of the ordinary. When I finished the hardware, Wes set up a saw in one of the apartments so I could cut the door casing to length. This is mind-numbing repetitive work; the casing is cut and the extra piece is thrown away. I dragged the trash can to the saw, put on my headphones, and began— cut, throw away, cut, and throw away. I was the only one working in this apartment, but like Wes had complained of, I kept feeling as though someone was watching me.

When he and I left for lunch, I asked him if there was a reason he chose to have me work out of that particular apartment. Before I could say anything else he said, "You felt it! Didn't you?"

I had felt as though someone was watching me, but I also thought that maybe all of Wes's talk about the place being haunted was just getting to me. Our roles had definitely switched, and not wanting to encourage him in his craziness, I changed the subject.

After lunch, I returned to the saw. Cut, throw away, cut, and throw away. After working awhile, I noticed that a pile of the scrap pieces had missed the trash can. I turned off the saw, picked up the pieces, moved the trash can closer, and started again. Later, glancing at the floor, I saw another pile lying beside the trash can.

How hard can it be to hit the trash can? It's right next to me. After cleaning up the mess, I started again. This time I watched the pieces as I tossed them into the can. One after the other they landed in the can. But then, one of them floated out. It clearly went into the can, came back out, and landed on the floor. Then it happened again. I threw them softer thinking maybe they were bouncing out. But it didn't seem to matter how I threw them, every fourth or fifth piece came floating back out. Watching this over and over made me reconsider what Wes had said about this place being haunted.

Finishing the task and knowing Wes wasn't quite ready to leave for the day, I decided to do a little investigating. I sat down on a stack of wood and tried to clear my mind as Ken and Carroll had taught us to do. After making sure no one else was around, I whispered, "Is there someone in here with me?"

I had gotten impressions before, but never like this. Typically, I would get a sense of whether the ghost was a man or woman, but usually not much more than that. This time the information rushed in so quickly I had trouble processing it. I felt this ghost was an older man and his name was Albert. I felt that, at one time, he worked as the maintenance man for this apartment complex and the new tools of his old trade intrigued him. Even though I hadn't seen him, I had a clear picture in my mind of what Albert looked like.

It seemed as though I had some apologizing to do, so on our way home, I told Wes about my experience. He was thrilled. As it turned out, he was a little concerned about his sanity, too. But having someone else feel what he had felt made both of us learn to trust his judgment a little more.

Even though it was hard for me to get used to Wes talking about ghosts to our friends, family, and co-workers, I enjoyed the fact that he and I could talk about them together. This was a new experience. We frequently talked about the ghosts in our home, and Albert was usually the topic of our conversation on the way home from work.

With only a few weeks left before we finished the apartment job, Wes accepted a large order for some end tables. We decided he would continue at the apartments and I would work on the tables at the shop. Packing my tools at the end of the day, I commented to Wes that I was going to miss Albert. He laughed and told me to tell Albert not to be following him around once I left because it still kind of "creeped" him out.

I told Wes that Albert could come home with me, because I got lonely working by myself. Of course, I was kidding when I made that comment, but apparently Albert didn't know that.

2006–2007

....

Wes went back to work at the apartments while I stayed at the shop to build the tables. My first project was making the table rungs. I had to cut and sand hundreds of them. After working for a day and a half, I had almost completed step one.

As I tried to finish, I felt someone walk up behind me. Thinking it was Wes, I continued to work, but wondered why he was home so early. After a minute or two, I felt him breathing on the back of my neck. I turned the sander off and whirled around so I could adequately gripe at him.

There was no one there.

rungs, I carried them to a nearby table. For ease of counting, I stacked them in rows of twenty. When I returned to the sanding table, one of the neatly stacked piles of wood toppled over. As I watched, another pile fell, and then another. There was no reason these stacks should have fallen. As I made my way back to the table to restack them, I heard a faint shuffling sound as if someone was walking while dragging their feet. I stopped and called out, "Albert, is that you?" Immediately, one of the rungs floated up into the air and glided across the remaining stacks of wood. It hovered for a few seconds then landed with a thud on the table. My question was sufficiently answered.

We'd never had any paranormal activity at the new shop. We couldn't say that anymore. After Wes had finished the job at the apartments, he returned to work at the shop. He had his encounters with Albert, too. First, he saw what he described as a black mass moving across the back of the shop. A few days later he saw a black shadow in the shape of a man walk the length of the shop before disappearing.

It took awhile for Wes and I to get used to having Albert at the shop, but eventually we learned to not only accept him, but to look forward to seeing what he was going to do next. However, not everyone shared our sentiments.

Albert had been a resident at our shop for over a year before he made himself known to people other than Wes and me. My dad was the first of those lucky few. One Saturday afternoon, Wes and my dad were using the shop to work on Troy's car. They had been at the shop working most of the day when they stopped to take a break. As they were talking about their next move to fix the car, they saw the head of an eight-pound sledgehammer skid across the floor. Dad had heard Wes and me talk about our ghosts before, but he had never witnessed any of the activity.

Watching this heavy chunk of metal come to a stop, Dad scratched his head and looked over at Wes. When Wes told him he didn't think they were alone, Dad picked up his coffee mug and said he thought they should continue their break inside of the house. But Albert wasn't finished introducing himself just yet.

Because of the heavy workload, Wes hired a young man who was willing to work at the shop or on the job sites. One morning, he and Wes were working in the shop while I was enjoying a day off. Discovering they needed some supplies, Bryan agreed to stay while Wes made a trip into town.

Wes had been gone for about an hour when he called me at the house and asked me if I'd go check on Bryan. My first thought was that he had been hurt. Rushing to the door with the phone to my ear, I asked Wes what had happened.

Now laughing, Wes assured me he was fine. He explained Bryan had been spooked by something at the shop and he refused to go back into the building alone. As I walked to the shop, I wondered what could have happened to scare him bad enough for him to refuse to go back to work.

Laughing myself, I walked around the corner and saw Bryan sitting on the step in front of the shop. I quit laughing. Bryan's face was pale and his hands were visibly shaking. Not wanting to embarrass him, I just told him Wes had called and asked me to go check on him.

Bryan wiped the sweat from his forehead as he told me he knew Wes was probably laughing at him, but at this point, he didn't care. Showing no signs of embarrassment, he pointed a shaking finger at the shop and told me he wasn't going back in there by himself.

After I asked him to tell me what happened, he said he didn't even know how to explain it, but he hadn't been alone in the shop. He said he kept hearing all sorts of shuffling noises. When he told me he could feel someone breathing on the back of his neck, I knew he'd met Albert. Bryan continued telling me about his experience by explaining he had tried convincing himself it was just his imagination, but then he heard a loud bang and he just couldn't take it anymore.

I wasn't sure what to say. I knew Bryan believed in ghosts because the topic had come up when Wes showed him the picture of Christopher, but I also knew he was terrified of them. I tried to come up with other explanations for the things he'd experienced. I suggested maybe the shop had mice and that was what was causing some of the noise.

He drew in a ragged breath and said it hadn't been a mouse and he could guarantee that. He stood up and started pacing back and forth in front of the shop. He told me we could fire him if we wanted to, but he'd never work alone in the shop again.

Bryan was a good worker and I didn't want to lose him. I told him we weren't going to fire him. We'd work something out. Watching him pace back and forth, I finally suggested we go into the shop together. Bryan shook his head. Thinking he might need some time alone, I left him outside as I went into the shop.

It took ten minutes or so for Bryan to join me. When he walked in, he stood at the door and nervously looked around. He walked in a little further and shivered as he told me he didn't know what had been in there, but something had been.

I told him I'd stay and work with him until Wes got back. I picked up the broom and started sweeping. Bryan went back to his table and tried to work. Every few seconds I'd see him rub the back of his neck and turn around. He finally gave up; walking up to me, he said he knew that I believed in ghosts. He took a deep breath and asked if anything weird like this had happened in the shop before.

I was beginning to understand that not only was he scared of what had happened, but he also needed someone to believe and understand what he'd experienced. I could relate to these feelings very well so I told him the story of Albert.

"No, no, no," he said, "I just can't do this."

As I tried to reassure him, I heard Wes pull into the drive. I met him at the truck and quickly explained what had happened. I told him if he didn't want to lose Bryan as an employee he'd better not tease him.

When Wes walked into the shop, Bryan told him to go ahead and laugh because he knew he was going to. Wes told him he wasn't going to laugh at him because he knew firsthand what a pest Albert could be, but there could be another explanation for what Bryan had experienced. As Wes walked around, he stopped in front of a lawn tractor we had stored in the back end of the shop. He noticed the blade was on the ground. He always kept the blade up. Using the lever, he put it in the upright position then let it fall.

Bryan jumped. He told Wes that was the exact noise he had heard earlier. Feeling a little better about things, he asked if the blade could have fallen on its own.

Wes told him not unless he had bumped it. Bryan stared at the tractor. He told Wes that he hadn't been anywhere close to it. He paced the shop again and said that even if he had, that wouldn't explain the breathing on his neck. Shaking his head, he reiterated that he was never going to work by himself in the shop again.

We all agreed if Wes had to be away from the shop that I'd work with Bryan or he could have the day off. This, after all, wasn't the first time we'd had to make concessions for one of our ghosts.

22: BLIND EYES

2007

....

Talking to Bryan about Albert made me a little uncomfortable, but once I got used to the idea of not having to make excuses for our ghosts, it was quite appealing. I still wasn't comfortable bringing the subject up, but I'd decided if anything else were to happen, whether at the shop or even in our home, I'd let people draw their own conclusions.

In the past, if our guests witnessed paranormal activity, I had a list of "explanations" I'd fall back on. I usually blamed noises and the opening and closing of doors on the house settling. If a light turned off and on, that, of course, could be faulty wiring. The shadows were a little harder. Depending on the time of day, I sometimes blamed them on a moving branch outside the window. Even though I chose my words carefully, using phrases like "it could have been" or "maybe it was," I felt dishonest.

I was happy with my decision to let people come to their own conclusions and it amazed me to see just how many things people were willing to ignore. Seeing this time and time again has caused me to believe many people experience paranormal activity without ever acknowledging it.

I witnessed this mindset a couple of times when I was remodeling my bedroom. This project was supposed to be a simple one. I was going to repaint my walls and ceiling—that's all—period. Trying one of the new faux techniques on my walls, I accidently spilled half a gallon of paint on my carpet. This, of course, blew my budget. We had to purchase a new carpet. Trying to make it as cheap as possible, we made a deal with the carpet store. They said they would give us a discount if we emptied the room of all furniture and took out the old carpet.

With the furniture and carpet gone, we waited for the carpet installers. Day one, they never showed. Day two, they at least called to say it would be the next day before they could make it out. Even though the contents of my room were strung throughout the house, Keshia decided to invite a girlfriend over.

As the three of us sat in the living room and talked, we heard a crash and the sound of breaking glass come from my bedroom. We jumped up, weaved our way around the bedroom furniture and went into my room. A candle in a glass votive had fallen off a shelf and crashed onto the uncarpeted floor. We cleaned up the mess and went back into the living room. About thirty minutes later, we heard another crash. As before, the three of us went to my room. When we walked in, we saw the matching votive broken on the floor.

If this had happened only once, we probably wouldn't have thought too much about it. But happening twice, for no apparent reason, caused Keshia and I to exchange knowing looks with one another. Her friend didn't necessarily believe in ghosts, but she knew we did. Seeing the look that passed between Keshia and me, she shuddered. At first, she tried to come up with reasons as to why these candles would have fallen. Not believing the reasons herself, she chose to "just forget about it."

The next day when the carpet installer came, Wes took him to our room. As they stood in the center of the bedroom, one of the kids' bronzed baby shoes that was on a shelf came flying across the room and landed on the floor. Wes said the man jumped, but then just went right on with the conversation as if nothing had happened.

Letting people come to their own conclusions about the activity at our house not only took the pressure off me, but it also allowed me to see the many different viewpoints people had concerning ghosts. Most of our company consisted of friends of the children, who in actuality weren't children anymore. By this time, Keshia was in college and Troy was a senior in high school.

Keshia had chosen a college close to home, which allowed her to live with us while attending school. This was the perfect arrangement except for the fact that her fiancé, Stephen, lived three and a half hours away. Wanting to get to know the young man who'd won our daughter's heart, Wes and I had no problem with allowing him to spend some weekends with us. Thankfully, Keshia had already approached the subject of ghosts with him. Stephen believed in ghosts, but hadn't had many experiences himself. That, of course, was about to change.

We had a large sectional sofa in our living room, which served as Stephen's bed when he spent the night. He'd gotten in the habit of sleeping on one end of the couch. Where he lay, he could see down one of our hallways. Apparently one night after everyone had gone to bed, Stephen saw a light in the computer room turn on. As he lay looking down the hall, he watched it go off, back on, and back off.

The next morning he told Keshia what had happened. She assured him this type of activity wasn't unusual for our house. The next night as he prepared his bed on the couch, Keshia noticed he put his pillow on the other end. When she asked him why he was switching, he told her he knew we had ghosts, but he didn't have to watch them while he was trying to go to sleep. On another one of Stephen's visits, Keshia and the ghosts decided to have a little fun at his expense.

Since they didn't get to see each other often, they would stay up talking most of the night when Stephen did stay over. At some point after Wes and I had gone to bed, Keshia heard whispers coming from our room. At first, she thought we were still awake, but then she heard Wes snoring. Deciding to ignore it, she continued talking to Stephen.

It wasn't long before Stephen noticed the whispering as well. When he commented that her parents were up later than normal. She pretended not to know what he was talking about: Keshia pointed out that Wes was snoring. Stephen then asked who was whispering, and my sweet daughter told him that he was either crazy or hearing things.

Soon the whispering moved into a different part of the house. When Keshia insisted she didn't hear anything, Stephen got up to find the source. After allowing him to search for several minutes, she finally admitted that she'd heard the whispering all along, and that it was probably just the ghosts. Satisfied that he wasn't going crazy, Stephen sat back down, and soon afterward, the ghosts got bored and left them alone.

Upon hearing the story the next morning, I knew Stephen would fit into our family just fine.

23: GONE

2007

....

Living with ghosts for so many years, we'd all come to learn that any type of change in our home could cause a rise in activity. Whether it was a remodel, the birth of a child, or even something as minor as getting new furniture, the ghosts let us know that they noticed the transformation.

Our home was about to undergo one of the biggest changes yet. Our son, our baby, was moving away to attend college. As mothers tend to do, I had a mommy meltdown. Once Troy officially moved out, I cried and cried for days. Any mention of his name would bring me to tears. Of course, if his name wasn't mentioned, that also made me cry. After days of this, I decided the best thing for me to do was work. That's how I handle stress. I work. The harder the work, the better off I am.

Unfortunately, Wes had nothing for me to do on the job, so I was left to my own devices. With the yard mowed and the gardens weeded, the biggest, hardest, most difficult task I could think of was cleaning Troy's room. But when I went into his room I knew this wasn't a good idea at all. No doubt the room needed to be cleaned, but I couldn't do it—not yet. I left his room and vowed to get to it soon, but not that day. Closing his door behind me, I tackled cleaning out the cabinets, wallpapering the kitchen, and rearranging the living room.

I knew Wes and Keshia would be coming home any minute, so I tried to put on a happy face and pretend I wasn't going to die soon. Despite my best efforts, they knew all wasn't well on the home front.

Both of them crept around the house as if they were walking on eggshells. This only served to irritate me. "I'm okay!" I yelled. "Would you two quit looking at me like you think I'm going to crumble to the floor?" They slunk off in opposite directions. Fine, I thought. *Where's my family when I need them? Gone! Everybody's gone. Troy's gone. You guys won't talk to me! I'm all alone!* This of course brought on a new round of tears, sending me to the bathroom for more Kleenex. Walking down the hall, I noticed Troy's bedroom door was open. I slammed it shut. "Who keeps opening this door?" I yelled out. "I want it left closed!"

The next day wasn't much better, nor was the day after. My sisters, having already gone through this, tried to console me. It didn't work. Obviously, I loved my children more than my sisters loved theirs. They were still alive after their children had left home and I knew I wouldn't be able to survive much longer.

Knowing there was nothing left to scrub, polish, vacuum, or paint, I decided the time had come to take on the room—Troy's room. I walked down the hall with trash bags in tow and stopped in front of his open door. The same door I'd closed at least five times a day since he'd left.

I began picking up things in his discarded piles and shoving them into the bags. There were old clothes, torn football cards, and long-forgotten homework assignments. Little by little, the floor started to become visible. When I picked up his ripped football practice shirt, I couldn't believe he'd put it into the pile to be thrown away. True, I must've told him a hundred times to throw it away, but seeing it tossed aside was like closing the book on an era of our lives. There'd be no more Friday night high school football games. There'd be no more ... many things.

The familiar lump formed in my throat. Holding the threadbare shirt to my chest, I walked to his bed. I sat down and sobbed into his shirt. As I cried, I felt someone pat my back. Lifting my head from the now-wet shirt, I felt it again. There was no one there. Exhausted, I curled up on his sheetless bed and went to sleep as someone I couldn't see continued to pat my back.

After getting that day behind me, I started to see that perhaps my sisters were right. I might pull through. It was somehow possible to live with a heart that was broken into a million little pieces. Troy was less than two hours away and he'd promised to come home often. When he couldn't make it home for the weekend, I could always go and see him.

Surviving on these visits, I began looking forward to his Christmas break. When he called and asked me if I'd go shopping for his new girlfriend with him, I jumped at the chance. We scheduled our shopping excursion for his first day home.

Sticking with tradition, Keshia went shopping with Wes to insure my Christmas gifts wouldn't consist of power tools. She and Wes got in one vehicle while Troy and I got in another and we all headed out in separate directions. I had my son back and all to myself for awhile. We shopped, went out to dinner, and tried to catch up on each other's lives.

When Troy and I returned home, we saw that Wes and Keshia were still gone. I stood on the porch rummaging through my purse to find my house key while Troy impatiently jiggled the doorknob. As he backed away to let me insert the key, the door unlocked and opened wide. Startled, Troy turned and looked at me. I told him it appeared I wasn't the only one missing him.

He smiled and told me he hadn't seen anything and I hadn't either.

After putting our packages away, I watched Troy lock the front door as he went outside. When he began jiggling the doorknob, I knew what he was doing. He was his father's son. I watched him through the glass of the door. He jiggled the knob, he pushed on the door, and he jiggled some more. He looked up and saw that I was watching him; he smiled and told me to let him in. When I opened the door, he walked in, shrugged his shoulders, and said, "It's the wind."

My son was home!

Before we knew it, Troy's first year of college was over. My sisters were right. Somehow, I had survived.

Growing tired of dorm life, Troy called and wanted us to come help him move into a house he'd found. When we walked into his new place, it reminded me of the first time I had walked into my house so many years before. This house was not empty. There was someone here. As I walked around, I felt as though the presence was a male entity. It wasn't anything to be afraid of, so knowing how Troy felt about these things, I kept the impressions to myself. After helping Troy get settled in, Wes and I headed home. As we got into the car, Wes said he didn't think Troy was *alone.*

Wes told me when he was walking down the hall, he could feel someone following him. We discussed how we thought this was going to be an interesting move for Troy. Knowing how he felt about ghosts, we were curious to see how it was going to unfold. We both thought if Troy did ever notice anything, we'd never hear a word about it.

We were wrong. Troy was good about calling home and, during these calls, he'd talk about how he could hear someone walking around late at night. It was hard to keep my suspicions to myself, but I tried. At first, I told him it could be the house settling and that he just needed to get used to being somewhere different.

The longer Troy lived there, the longer his list of complaints became. He still talked about hearing someone walk around, but now he also talked about how, after locking his doors, he kept finding one of them unlocked.

When I finally shared my thoughts about his house, they were received with an, "Aw, Mom! It's just a creepy old house." Not expecting anything different, I told him I knew how he felt, so I would drop it.

Trying to stay true to my word, every time he called with a new story, I tried to come up with a reasonable explanation. He started complaining that when he got up in the mornings, he found his pots and pans stacked in the middle of the kitchen floor. I suggested maybe he had a squirrel or something in his cabinet and it pushed the pans out.

He told me he didn't think that could be the reason because they weren't scattered around, they were always stacked in the middle of the floor. Troy wanted to tell me about these incidents, but he'd always end with, "It's just a creepy old house." Then he'd want to change the subject.

One time, Keshia spent the night with Troy. When she came home, she told me Troy's house was so active, she didn't know how he could sleep at night. She went on to say she could hear someone walking, and pans rattling all night long. She said the rattling got so loud that she got up to see what was going on. She couldn't see anything unusual when she walked into the kitchen, but she could detect which cabinet the noise was coming from. When she opened the cabinet door, the noise stopped. She saw the cabinet only contained plastic—nothing that would have warranted the noise she heard.

A few days later, I was talking to Troy on the phone and he told me he needed to find another house because it was impossible to sleep there. He said in addition to hearing someone walk around and pots and pans rattling, now his washing machine was turning itself on in the middle of the night.

As I tried to stammer out possible reasons for this to happen, Troy said, "Cut the crap, Mom. We both know this place is haunted!"

I laughed. "Okay but I thought you didn't believe in ghosts."

"Well...I don't...most of the time."

24: WEDDING BELLS

2008–2009

....

If anyone's ever told you it gets easier to watch your children leave home after the first one, they lied. A year after Troy moved out, Keshia, my firstborn, my only daughter, started planning her wedding. Sure, she'd done as I'd asked; she was waiting until after she graduated college and she even gave me a year's notice before the wedding. But still ... my daughter ... getting married; I didn't know how much more my heartstrings could take.

Apparently, my children had more confidence in me and in my heartstrings than I did. Just as Keshia and I started making arrangements for her wedding, Troy came home with a little news of his own. He was about to propose to his girlfriend. "But ... but ... but ... " I stammered. "You can't get married. Your sister is getting married."

Troy put his arm around my shoulders and told me not to worry. His wedding would be long after Keshia's.

After the proposal, the wedding date was set. Troy was right. His wedding would take place after Keshia's—by two months. That's right, two formal weddings in two months! "No, no, no, I can't do this! We can't have two weddings—two months apart."

"Sure we can." Troy beamed. "Besides, you're exaggerating. My wedding will be two months and a day after Keshia's."

Well, that makes all the difference in the world. Let's see, Keshia will graduate college. Two weeks later, she'll get married. Two months—and a day—later Troy will get married. Graduation, two weddings, less than a year away, two months apart! Deep breath in and slowly let it out.

It's a good thing work helps me deal with stress, because that year consisted of a lot of both. Between the dinners, the luncheons, the showers, and the wedding planning, I walked around in a daze. Before I knew it, wedding number one was fast approaching. It was all so exciting, exhausting ... and sad. I absolutely adored my new soon-to-be son- and daughter-in-law, but still ... How had my own children grown up so fast?

Keshia's moving out was different from Troy's, not easier as I'd been told it would be, but different. When

Troy left, it was all done and over with in one single heart-wrenching day. With Keshia, the pain was drawn out s-l-o-w-l-y. Now that Stephen had moved closer, she began taking some of her things, little by little, to his apartment. It was like having my life's blood drained one agonizing drop at a time.

During one these bloodletting sessions, Stephen came over to help Keshia haul away more of her things. Trying to lighten my sour mood, I decided to pick on him a little bit by telling him to be sure and take some of the ghosts with him because I didn't want Keshia to miss her friends. Stephen laughed and said she would just have to come home to visit them because he didn't want them at his house.

I quietly feared Stephen might not get his wish. We had a few ghosts that were attached to Keshia and I thought they would follow her wherever she went. I was right. Within a day or two of moving some of Keshia's things into his apartment, he complained about "weird stuff" happening.

It's said that a girl tends to marry someone like her father. In Keshia's case, this was proving to be true. Even though Stephen did at least believe in ghosts, he wasn't ready to admit he might be living with one, so he tried to come up with other reasons for the things he was experiencing. The first thing he tried to figure out was why a door on his bathroom cabinet was always open. After checking that the latch worked properly, he decided

Keshia must be leaving it open to "mess with him." Stephen is six feet two inches compared to Keshia's five feet, so he said she was leaving the door open because she knew he would hit his head on it. Keshia told him that she would have done it if she'd thought of it, but that did nothing to convince him of her innocence. When he continued to find the door open on the days she hadn't come over, while also noticing that one of his bedroom doors kept opening and closing on its own, he knew his excuses were running out.

Even though it was becoming apparent some of our ghosts were hanging out at Stephen's place, we still had a few of our own. A day or two before the wedding, Keshia called me to her room. When I walked in, I saw she was packing more of her things. I was about to ask what she needed, but before I had the chance to speak, I got a strong whiff of wonderfully fragrant perfume. I didn't recognize the scent, so I asked her what kind it was.

She told me that was why she called me in there. She was hoping I recognized the fragrance because it wasn't hers. She asked if I could still smell it. I sniffed the air, but the scent had already disappeared.

Phantom smells weren't uncommon in our house. Typically, these unaccounted-for aromas came from the kitchen. In times past, the scent of freshly baked bread, frying bacon, and even the stench of burnt beans had wafted through our house unaccounted for, but we'd never smelled this perfume before.

The big day arrived and the wedding couldn't have gone any better. The decorations were elegant, the food was delectable, the cake was beautiful—and delivered on time. And the bride ... well ... she was positively radiant! Oh, I know a lot of mothers use words such as radiant, breathtaking, and stunning to describe their daughters on their wedding day, but Keshia truly was. Her gown fit perfectly, and her long, beautiful hair hung in curls, but it was her smile I couldn't get over. Her smile did more than light the room, it lit my heart. Her smile made it almost impossible to be sad. Looking at her, I thought I might survive this after all. That was until Stephen's car pulled away, with my daughter in it.

Work, I needed to work! There was so much to be done. The church building had to be cleaned, the dishes washed, the decorations taken down and packed. There was so much to do, I didn't know if I'd ever get done. But I did. And the emptiness set in. My daughter was gone!

After we got home, I started carrying the boxes of keepsakes to her room—what used to be her room. *I can't do this.* I thought. *Not again, not now, I need a little more time.* Looking around the room, my mind took me back to happier times. I remembered the nighttime prayers, the bedtime stories, the hugs and kisses, the ...

Interrupting my thoughts, Wes came in carrying another box of wedding memorabilia. He asked me where I wanted it.

I dabbed at my eyes and told him it didn't matter.

"Lisa," he said. "It's going to be okay."

I had somehow held it together all day. I'd even managed not to throw myself down the aisle as she walked down it. But this...no, I couldn't handle this. Not the husky, "I'm about to cry myself, our baby girl's gone, what are we going to do now?" kind of voice. No, not that!

As we held each other in the center of our daughter's empty room, Wes asked me if I was wearing a new perfume.

I lifted my tear-soaked face from his shoulder and again smelled that wonderful scent I'd noticed a few days earlier. Wiping my eyes, I shook my head.

He drew in a deep breath and said he could've sworn he smelled perfume, but now he couldn't. I told him he had smelled perfume—and even though our home was officially empty of children, it wasn't empty of ghosts.

25: MOVING ON

2009

....

The human heart is a miraculous organ. Even though it's only roughly the size of a clenched fist, on average it beats seventy-two times a minute. That's every minute of every day for the duration of our lives—even when it's broken. With both of my children married in the span of two months, I knew this to be true because I'd somehow survived both weddings.

Troy's wedding was as beautiful as Keshia's had been. With the church building once again decorated and full of family and friends, I watched my son, my baby, say, "I do." The wedding couldn't have gone any better and Troy, well, he was the most handsome of all grooms.

Life was moving fast. Troy not only had a new wife, but a new house as well. He'd purchased his first house right before the wedding and as far as we could tell, his new house was free of ghosts.

That was not the case with Keshia and Stephen. The ghost or ghosts that had taken up residence with Stephen were still there.

Keshia and Stephen lived close by and they were good about coming over to visit. After leaving our house one evening, Keshia called me when they got back to their apartment. She told me Stephen wanted her to call and say thank you.

Always being grateful for gratitude, I told her to tell him he was welcome. I then asked what he was thanking me for.

She laughed as she told me that maybe the words "thank you" weren't quite right. She said it was more like, "We can thank your Mom for this!"

Keshia explained that, since they were saving money for a down payment on a house, she had been complaining to Stephen about him leaving the lights on. When they got home from our house, they noticed a light shining through the living room window. Keshia had been the last one to leave, so Stephen was now giving her a hard time about their high electric bill.

As they walked up to the door, they noticed the light was giving off an orange glow. They couldn't decide which one of their lights would do this, but once they unlocked the door and went in, the apartment was completely dark. There were no lights on anywhere.

My protective radar kicked in. I asked her if she was certain no one was in the apartment. Easing my fears, she told me they had checked the entire apartment and no one was there. She said they had locked both doors before leaving and both doors were still locked when they got home.

I could hear Stephen laughing and talking in the background. He was saying if I hadn't told him to take some of the ghosts with him then none of this would be happening.

None of this… hmmm. I asked Keshia what other types of activity she'd witnessed at the apartment. She said there was the "normal stuff," like hearing footsteps and seeing doors open and close on their own.

Who, but my daughter, would consider this normal? It struck me then how un-normal her life truly had been. Keshia had lived with and acknowledged ghosts her entire life. I knew all marriages came with a certain amount of baggage, I just hoped Stephen was okay with Keshia's baggage being ghosts.

I asked her how Stephen was handling all of this. She said he was getting used to it, but the incident with the shishi dogs had sort of freaked him out.

Not even knowing what a shishi dog was, I knew this was a story I wanted to hear. She explained that these were small statues from Japan. It is believed that shishi dogs protect from spirits. One dog welcomes good spirits while the other one guards against evil ones.

I couldn't imagine why Stephen would even have something like that until Keshia explained one of his friends had gone to Japan and bought them for Stephen as a souvenir. She said that guys were weird; they couldn't buy each other normal souvenirs like bracelets or t-shirts, but spirit guardian dogs were acceptable.

Then she told me that upon returning home from work one day she found one of the dogs across the room from where it was supposed to be. It was the dog that was meant to guard against evil spirits.

Keshia was used to things being rearranged, so she didn't think too much about it. Stephen, on the other hand, was a little upset thinking about who ... or what ... had moved the dog. He also wondered if there was any significance in the fact that the dog that was moved was the one to guard against evil spirits.

In my own experiences, I'd never met a ghost I would consider evil. I'm not saying they don't exist, but if the ghost now living with Keshia was one of ours, I didn't think Stephen had anything to worry about.

I was never able to determine which of our ghosts had left. What I did know was our home was as active as ever.

Keshia's room had always had a lot of activity and her moving out hadn't changed that.

One morning while taking my shower, I heard what sounded like furniture moving around in Keshia's old room. She'd left a few things, but I didn't know she was coming to get them. I turned the shower off and yelled out that I'd be out in a minute. As I dried off, I wondered what she was looking for. It sounded as though she was going through her dresser and slamming each drawer.

Just as I was about to open the bathroom door, I heard another loud bang. Whatever had caused that noise visibly shook the bathroom wall. I yelled out and asked her what she was doing. There was no answer. It occurred to me she should be at work by this time of the morning. If it wasn't her, who was in my house?

Cold fear ran through me as I wondered if an intruder had come into the house. I looked around the bathroom for something I could use as a weapon. I didn't find anything suitable, so I grabbed the shampoo thinking I could at least rub it in someone's eyes if I had too. I heard another loud noise and, armed with my bottle of shampoo, I quietly opened the door and peered down the hall.

Her bedroom door was closed. I called out her name again. In response, there was another bang. With my heart racing, I crept to her door, gently opened it, and looked inside. All was quiet and the room was neat and orderly. As I walked further into the room, I saw a mist at the foot of her bed. This mist didn't really have a specific shape.

It just looked like a patch of fog, a vertical patch of fog. As I stood there watching it, it started to dissipate and I could smell the scent of that wonderful perfume. Leaving the room and closing the door, I again heard the sound of furniture moving across the floor.

A few days later, I was in the computer room chatting online with Susan, the woman I'd met at the seminar. I started hearing the sound of furniture moving around in Keshia's room again. I didn't want to interrupt our conversation, so I ignored it for a time. The noise grew so loud and intense, I again started to wonder if someone was in the house.

Typing into the chat box, I explained what was happening and told Susan I'd be right back. The noise grew louder as I walked towards Keshia's room. Even though her room is carpeted, it sounded as though furniture was sliding across a hardwood floor. As soon as I stepped into the hallway, the noise stopped. I opened her door and everything looked as it should.

I went back to the computer to continue my conversation with Susan. Within a few minutes, the noise started again. I could hear the furniture sliding, the dresser drawers slamming, and the sound of something hitting the wall. I described the activity to Susan; she suggested I go take some pictures.

I disconnected from the Internet and found my camera. The noise intensified. With camera in hand and intent on my mission, I was hurrying through the living room when Wes opened the front door.

I screamed.

The noise stopped.

Shocked at his welcome, he asked what was going on.

With my heart slamming in my chest, question after question tumbled out of my mouth. I demanded to know when he got home, what he was doing, how long he had been there and, most importantly, if he was responsible for all the noise I'd been hearing.

Taking my hand, he told me to slow down and tell him what was going on.

I took a deep breath and explained what had been happening. Wes and I tiptoed into Keshia's room—her quiet, orderly room. There was no mess, no noise, no fragrance, and no mist.

It had been a long time since I'd felt like Wes didn't believe me. But I could tell by his expression that he at least thought I was exaggerating. It wasn't long, however, until he experienced this noisy ghost for himself.

A few days later, Wes was working in the house, catching up on some paperwork, while I went outside to do some gardening. I'd been outside thirty minutes or so when he came out and asked me what I had been doing to make so much noise in Keshia's room.

When I told him I hadn't been in the house, he looked confused. He said he had gone into the bathroom and while he was in there he heard what sounded like furniture being moved and dresser drawers slamming shut. After checking for himself to make sure Keshia's old room was in order, he too came to the conclusion that the empty rooms in our house were still occupied.

2009

....

Becoming empty nesters left Wes and me with the task of deciding what to do with the children's rooms. It seemed as though we'd spent the majority of our married lives trying to make the house big enough to accommodate our family of four. Now we had more room than the two of us needed and the recently vacated bedrooms were unused. We talked about converting Troy's room into another home office, and replacing Keshia's twin-sized bed with a double bed and turning her room into a guest room.

Being a "clean freak," as my children so often put it, I did go into their rooms occasionally to dust and vacuum.

Going into Troy's room, I'd find exactly what you'd expect from an unoccupied room—nothing. Going into Keshia's room was a little different. Someone was in there and whoever it was made me uncomfortable. It seemed as though the ghost would stand where I'd stand. It would walk where I'd walk. Even though the room was empty, it felt crowded. I kept thinking whoever was in there thought I was invading Keshia's privacy. These feelings never manifested into anything more. That is, until I spent the night there.

Wes was working so many hours that his snoring was out of control. Lying awake in bed one night with the trainlike snoring roaring in my ears, I grabbed my pillow and went to Keshia's room. By this time, it was about two o'clock in the morning and I was exhausted. I turned down the sheets and fell into her bed.

We didn't have air-conditioning in the back part of the house, and even though it was hot summertime, her room was cold. With only a sheet and light bedspread, I eventually started to shake. The temperatures had reached triple digits that day and I was freezing. Keshia used to say she had "ghost conditioning." I got up, retrieved a blanket from her closet, and went back to bed.

Snuggling under the blanket, I went to sleep. After being asleep for only a little while, I awoke with a jolt. I couldn't figure out why I had woken in such a panic. Just as I tried to get back to sleep, I felt a light push on my shoulder. I couldn't see anything in the dark, but I felt a hand grip my shoulder and give a much harder shove.

I bolted out of the bed and turned on the light. The words "You shouldn't be in here," repeated over and over in my head. I couldn't be sure if this was something I was picking up from the ghost. What I did know was that I wasn't about to sleep in that room. I took my pillow and went to the couch.

When it came time to clean the children's rooms again, I found myself putting off going into Keshia's room altogether. Postponing it as long as I could and knowing the dust bunnies must be taking over, I finally resolved to get it done. I started by dusting the furniture and by the time I was ready to vacuum, the daunting feelings had returned. I finished as quickly as possible. Trying to make myself feel better, I looked around the empty room and said, "I have a right to be in here, you know. This is my house." I walked out and shut the door. Before I made it down the hall, I heard a loud thump against the wall. I picked up the pace and thought, *Okay, maybe I don't.*

A few days later Keshia and Stephen came over for dinner and I mentioned to her that I was uncomfortable going into her old room. I told her she should tell her "friends" that she'd moved and it was okay for me to be in there.

Even though I'd been joking when I told her to take care of the problem, I couldn't help but wonder if it might actually work. After all, my impression of the situation was that whoever was in there felt it was their responsibility to protect Keshia and her privacy.

A few days later, I decided to store some things in Keshia's closet; I stood outside the bedroom door, dreading to go in. I took a few deep breaths, squared my shoulders, held my head high, and marched in. Determined to accomplish my mission, I went straight to the closet. After putting a few boxes away, I went for another load, then another. I could tell there was a difference in the room. There was no fear, no uncomfortable feelings, and no thoughts of how I shouldn't be there.

I went back into her room the next day with the sole purpose of checking the "feel" of the room; I was again pleasantly surprised. There was someone in there but whoever it was no longer wanted me out. This I could live with. I didn't know what had brought about the change, but I was glad to see it.

A week or so passed by the next time Keshia and Stephen came over. As we sat and talked, I told her that I was thinking about re-texturing and painting her old room. She said if I was willing to spend that much time in there then her talk with the ghosts must have worked. I didn't know she'd actually done as I'd suggested, but now I understood why her room no longer scared me.

With the kids gone, I guess some of the ghosts had gotten bored with hanging out in the uninhabited part of the house because Wes and I started to see more activity in other rooms.

One thing we couldn't ignore was that one of the ghosts had taken to answering our phone. It had happened in the past, but never this frequently. At first, we thought we were just getting a lot of hang-up calls because the phone would ring and before we could get to it, it would quit. Hearing the ringing phone suddenly stop, we assumed the caller had hung up until the phone started making the annoying beep, beep, beep, sound as if it had been left off the hook.

After experiencing this multiple times, we got in the habit of picking up the phone even after it had stopped ringing. Usually the caller would still be on the line and would ask what had taken us so long to speak after we'd picked up the phone. Depending on the caller, we generally didn't offer to tell them we weren't the ones who had actually answered the phone.

The ghost could not only answer the phone, but could also hang it up. After all these years, my sister Wanda still called the same time every morning. Expecting her call, I normally answered the phone before the ghosts had a chance to beat me to it. Most mornings while we were talking, the phone would suddenly go dead. By looking at my phone, I could see it wasn't a lost connection; the green light was off, signifying the phone had been hung up.

After this happened multiple times, I finally told her I thought the ghost was disconnecting our call. She'd long ago given up on getting me to move. She simply said she just didn't know how we could stay in *that* house.

The ghost took this game to another level by showing us it was capable of more than simply answering and
hanging up the phone. While working on the computer
one day I heard the phone ring. By finishing what I was
doing before answering the phone, I allowed the ghost to
get to it before I did. When I got to the phone, picked it
up, and said, "Hello," there was no one on the line. I put
the phone back in its cradle. As I walked off, it rang again.
When I picked it up, my sister Tammy asked why Wes had
hung up on her. She said she had just called the house and
Wes answered the phone, said hello, and hung up.

Wes was in the house, but he was in the bathroom. I
yelled out to him to see if he had answered the phone. He
hadn't. When I told Tammy it wasn't him, she asked who
else was at the house, because it sounded like Wes. She
went on to say the phone had rung several times when a
man answered, said hello, and promptly hung up.

Not being able to come up with any viable excuses, I
told her if a man had answered the phone, it must have
been one of our ghosts because there wasn't anyone else
at our house.

Like most of the family, Tammy knew we had ghosts,
but to have one actually talk to her was a new experience.
After stammering into the phone, she told me she would
never call my weird little house again.

Wes loved to give my sisters a hard time and now that
he was out of the bathroom and listening to the conversation, Wes said he loved having ghosts. He'd been trying

for years to get rid of the sisters-in-law and the ghost got rid of one of them with one little phone call.

Wes was intrigued with this phone-answering ghost. He told Charlie, one of his employees, all about it. Charlie believed in ghosts and had had quite a few experiences himself. Like us, he found the topic of ghosts fascinating, so we knew we didn't have to worry about the ghosts chasing him off. He'd already had a couple of experiences at the shop. He'd seen shadows and heard noises but had never been put off by it.

One day while working at the shop, he and Wes came to the house for their lunch break. After visiting with them for a while, I went back outside to work in the garden. As I worked, I heard the phone ring. Knowing Wes would answer it, I didn't rush in. I finished what I was doing and went inside to see who'd called. I found Charlie sitting alone at the dining room table finishing his lunch. I asked him where Wes was.

Charlie pointed down the hall and said he thought Wes was in the bathroom. Charlie said he'd thought about answering the phone, but it quit ringing after only two rings.

I then heard the beep, beep, beep. I turned to Charlie. He raised his eyebrows, then said, "What the ... ? Was that ... ?" He smiled. "Hey Wes," he hollered down the hall. "Your ghost is answering the phone again."

Wes had found a good employee in Charlie. He was a hard worker, and equally important around our home, he wasn't intimidated by ghosts.

27: UNANSWERED QUESTIONS

2009

....

With the kids out of the house, Wes and I had more time to pursue our interest in ghosts. With the use of e-mail, I continued my studies with Carroll Heath. As a clairvoyant, his methods of studying the paranormal were very different from the mainstream "ghost hunters." While these groups depended on their electronic equipment to detect the presence of ghosts, Carroll relied only on his senses.

Wes and I were interested in learning more about both methods. We read a lot of books, and continued to attend Ken and Carroll's yearly seminars. We found that by practicing meditation as they suggested, we were more sensitive to the presence of ghosts. However, being unsure of ourselves, we also found utilizing the digital camera and voice recorder often gave our experiences the validation we desired.

We decided to purchase an EMF detector to add to our equipment. EMF stands for electromagnetic field. With this instrument, it is possible to locate and track energy sources. Many people believe the presence of a ghost will disrupt this field and cause the meter to show higher-than-normal readings.

The EMF detector we purchased was specifically designed for paranormal investigators. The difference between this one and one an electrician might use is that the meter can be set to sound an alarm and/or blink if high-energy fields are detected.

After becoming familiar with the detector, we decided to take it with us on an upcoming trip. Wes and I were going to team up with Don and Susan to conduct an informal investigation of the Basin Springs Hotel. Like the Crescent, this historical hotel is also located in Eureka Springs, Arkansas and is rumored to be haunted.

We arrived at the Basin with our digital cameras, voice recorders, and EMF detector. The four of us met in the room Wes and I were staying in for the night. As we talked, we noticed a large cold spot move through the room. Wes, anxious to use the EMF detector, held it in the center of the cold spot. The meter shrieked its alarm. When he moved it away from the cold spot, it fell silent.

We couldn't find any electrical sources that might cause this, but the alarm continued to sound. Approximately thirty minutes into the investigation, the cold spot disappeared and the detector fell silent.

After investigating other areas of the hotel, Wes and I finally got into bed about one o'clock in the morning. Quickly falling asleep, I was jolted awake less than an hour later by feeling a sharp tug on my blanket. Wes was sleeping peacefully beside me. I felt a second and then a third tug on my blanket. I smelled the faint fragrance of perfume. I slipped out of bed and got the EMF detector. I put it on silent mode and laid it on the bedside table. It blinked, signifying a high reading. It stopped, and then started again. I watched the meter continue to blink for about twenty minutes with no discernable pattern. The meter stopped and the fragrance of perfume disappeared.

Our investigation of the Basin Hotel had been an exciting one. We all encountered the cold spot in the hotel room, my blanket was tugged, and we all heard unexplainable noises throughout the investigation. We all agreed that it was more than a rumor that the hotel was haunted.

I was moderately impressed with the EMF detector and I hoped it could be equally useful at home. The computer room was getting a lot of attention from at least one of our ghosts, which meant the room had our attention as well. At night, we would hear the sound of someone typing on the keyboard and drawers opening and closing. Walking into the room, we'd sometimes find the computer logged on to the Internet and occasionally we'd see blank sheets of paper shooting out of the printer. At first, I thought we must have a computer glitch, but when we started finding that the chair had moved to the opposite side of the room, I knew a ghost must have been responsible. I tried taking pictures and had spent countless hours trying to capture EVPs, all with no success.

Since the computer room served as a home office, I spent a lot of time in there during the day. Usually the only sign of paranormal activity was the feeling of being watched. At night, it was a different story. The noises would start and often continued until early morning. Since our bedroom was located right down the hall, this sometimes made sleep impossible.

Lying awake and listening to the noise coming from the computer room, I got the EMF detector. As I walked in, the room grew quiet. I could see the chair had been moved and even though the printer was off, there were several blank pieces of paper lying on the printer tray.

I turned the meter on and placed it on the desk. I sat quietly and waited. Nothing happened; the meter showed no activity and the room remained quiet. I'd learned that living with ghosts had its ups and downs. On the up side, our curiosity about their existence is continually being fed. On the down side, this feeding takes place on their schedule—not ours. With the meter still not showing any activity, it seemed as though this was going to be another failed attempt. Disappointed, I left the meter turned on and went back to bed.

I awoke about two hours later to the sound of the EMF detector sounding its alarm. I jumped up and ran into the computer room. I saw the red light flashing as the alarm continued to shriek. Looking at the meter, I saw the needle was showing its highest reading of five milligauss. As I stood staring at the meter, it dropped to a reading of zero and the alarm and flashing light stopped.

Witnessing this gave me even more confidence in the EMF detector, but in the end, it was just one more experience to go along with countless others. After living with ghosts for twenty-five years, I wanted more. I wanted to understand why the ghosts were here and I wanted to know why we had so much activity. Even though Wes and I tried to educate ourselves concerning ghosts, it seemed we still had more questions than answers.

28: PONDERINGS

2009

....

Even though I didn't know how Wes would feel about
it, I pondered the idea of having a professional paranormal group come to our home to conduct an investigation. I knew these groups had more experience and better equipment than I had and thought that perhaps they
could help answer some of my questions. With the World
Wide Web at my fingertips, I began researching the local
teams. Hoping to find a reputable group, I began famil-
iarizing myself with each one.

The Oklahoma Paranormal Research and Investigations team, better known as OKPRI, captured my interest.

This group had been investigating homes and businesses for over ten years and had been featured on several local and cable channels.

As I continued researching this group, the one thing that really got my attention was their definition of the word paranormal. They define it as "the normal not yet understood." Having encountered so many ghosts over the years, this simple definition spoke volumes to me.

While still researching this group, Keshia called and wanted Wes and me to come and look at a house she and Stephen were thinking about buying.

Putting my research aside, we promised to meet them there. Pulling into the drive, I was already impressed. It was easy to see this house, thank goodness, was much nicer than what Wes and I had started with. Trying to take it all in, I walked around the outside first. The yard was big and it was easy to see that at one time someone had taken great pride in it.

I was a little disheartened with the inside of the house. Apparently, whoever had lived here had taken better care of the outside than they had the inside. But at least this house had running water, and the walls weren't riddled with holes as ours had been. Listening to Keshia talk about her remodeling plans, my excitement returned.

As we continued to look around, OKPRI's definition, *the normal not yet understood*, spoke to me again. This house wasn't empty. I kept getting a prickly sensation on the back of my neck and I was sure an elderly male entity was following us around. My mind raced with questions, the most prevalent one being, *Exactly how normal was it to have ghosts?*

I knew Keshia had looked at this house several times before and she'd never mentioned to me that it had a ghost. While looking at the house, I could never find the time with her alone to ask her about it. The presence was strong and I kept thinking, *surely she knows—she has to feel it.* Preparing to leave, I had to be content with just telling her to call me later.

That evening when she called, she started the conversation by telling me they had made an offer on the house.

I knew Keshia wouldn't be bothered by the fact I thought the house had a ghost, but I wasn't quite sure how Stephen would feel. Since they'd already made an offer on the house, I decided to keep my thoughts to myself. After all, I wasn't an expert and if Keshia hadn't noticed it, maybe there hadn't been anything to notice. I wondered if researching paranormal groups earlier that day hadn't clouded my judgment.

We talked about the house and the improvements Keshia hoped to make. During the conversation, she kept asking me what I thought about the house. I talked about all the typical things one does when discussing purchasing a home. I mentioned the size of the house, the nice neighborhood, and how pretty the yard could be, but each point I brought up was met with her saying, "But what did you think about it?"

She obviously wanted me to say something, but I wasn't sure exactly what. Knowing she was excited, I brought up everything, both good and bad, I could think of. We discussed wall and carpet colors, appliances, and even possible furniture arrangements. I didn't know what else to say, so I was baffled when she asked me again what I thought about the house. Finally thinking I knew what she was getting at, I asked her if she was referring to the house, the yard, or to the ghost that came with it.

She laughed as she told me she had been wondering if I'd picked up on him.

Him, I thought. I didn't understand how, but we'd done it again. We'd both gotten the same impression from an entity we hadn't seen. It was definitely time to get some answers.

29: WAVERING

2009–2010

....

I continued to research the local paranormal groups and OKPRI was still my number-one choice. They were active in the community and frequently hosted public events. I attended one of these events and liked how they conducted their classes—I knew they were dedicated to trying to help others understand more about ghosts. It was obvious this group was passionate about what they did and the service they provided.

Like other groups, they utilized scientific methods to gather data for their investigations. If they found evidence of a haunting, whether it was pictures, voice recordings, or video, they'd pass this information and a copy of the findings on to their clients. Like the investigation itself, this came at no cost to the home or business owner.

Differing from some of the local groups, they also used psychics to aid them in their investigations. I was a little uncomfortable with this aspect. Even though I believed Carroll had this type of ability, I knew other people claimed to, but offered little to no proof. Since I can't explain how Keshia and I often receive the same impressions from ghosts, who am I to say what is and isn't possible?

Deciding OKPRI was the group I wanted to investigate our home, I talked it over with Wes and filled out the investigation request form online. Within a week, I received a phone call from Cathy Nance, the case manager.

Cathy was very professional and thorough. She asked a lot questions about our home and the activity we'd experienced. After talking for quite awhile, she told me our house was a case they'd be interested in investigating and I could expect Christy, the founder of the group, to call.

There were more calls over the next couple of weeks until the investigation was scheduled. As I wrote it on my calendar, the excitement began to build. I'd waited so long to do something like this, but along with the excitement came something I hadn't expected, nervousness.

I'd spent years trying to cover up the fact we had ghosts and now I'd invited a team of strangers into my home to look for them. I knew time had changed many people's perspective on ghosts, but a part of me still had the same old fears of not wanting to tell people my house was haunted.

Second-guessing my decision, I contemplated calling OKPRI and cancelling the investigation. On one hand, I desperately wanted answers and didn't know where else to get them. On the other, old fears are hard to lay aside. As the battle raged on in my mind, Keshia unknowingly helped me make my decision by remodeling her own haunted house.

Anxious to move into their new home, they started working on it before they signed the final papers. On top of their "to do" list was taking out the carpet and painting the walls. In the process, they discovered some crazy things previous homeowners had done. The first thing they found was that someone had laid carpet over carpet and in some cases, carpet over carpet over tile. Tearing out the layers, Stephen complained about whoever had done this.

As they continued working through their projects, Keshia got the impression that the entity wasn't too happy with all of their grumbling. After all, he was probably the one who'd done a lot of the things they were complaining about. As they worked on the house, Keshia made a conscious effort to keep her complaints to herself. She'd never been scared of ghosts, but she said this one made her a little uncomfortable and she didn't want to agitate him.

Soon after moving in, she and Stephen started to notice more and more activity. Apparently, like many men, this ghost took his TV time very seriously. If they were watching a show and decided to turn it off before the program was over, the TV would frequently come back on.

Each day, it seemed they gained a little more insight into the personality of the entity they now lived with. With a few bumps here and there, Keshia, Stephen, and the older male entity were learning to live peacefully together. Nighttime was probably the most difficult because the ghost would stand in the hall just outside their bedroom and Stephen complained that he could feel the entity staring at him, which made it difficult for him to go to sleep.

Because Keshia had lived with ghosts all of her life; she'd learned to tune them out when she needed to, but Stephen hadn't learned to do this yet. Lying in bed one night, feeling as though he was being watched, Stephen saw a movement across the hall in the bathroom. Seeing it several more times, he told Keshia about it. She looked across the hall and into the bathroom and confirmed that she saw it too. Despite the fact that the bathroom was dark, they could see a shadow moving around. She got bored with watching the shadow and rolled back over. Before getting to sleep, she heard Stephen exclaim, "I saw him! I saw his face!"

Keshia looked into the bathroom again, but this time she couldn't see anything. From her own experiences, she knew this was to be expected. If an entity chose to reveal himself, the image usually didn't last very long. Keshia had never seen the entity. She had, however, gotten impressions of what he looked like, so she asked Stephen to describe what he'd seen.

He told her the face was illuminated with light and that it reminded him of the character Gollum from the movie *Lord of the Rings.* Gollum is an almost skeletal-looking man with sparse hair and missing teeth. This description matched what Keshia had envisioned exactly.

After the latest of what had become almost daily "ghost reports" from Keshia, I had to suppress a shudder. Just because I'd had similar experiences myself didn't mean that sometimes these things didn't totally freak me out. It appeared Keshia's life was going to continue as it had started. Ghosts were going to be a part of it—but why?

The more I experienced, the more questions I had. My mind was made up. I wanted OKPRI to come to my house, and hopefully I could gain some insight.

30: OKPRI

2010

....

The weather we were experiencing the night of the investigation seemed to have been special-ordered for a horror movie. The moon was full and it eerily lit the fog that hung heavily over the house. Nearing the end of winter, it was already dark when the first member of OKPRI arrived around seven p.m. Shortly after, another one came, then another, then two more, and so on. I was surprised to see nine people show up for an investigation on my 1600-square-foot house, but it was obvious each person had a job to do.

Cathy first explained the process of how they conducted their investigations. She told us that Christy, the psychic, would want to do what she called a "cold walk-through" of the house. Christy preferred not to know about the activity we'd experienced, so she stayed outside while I took several members of the team through the house.

After the tour, the team began setting up their equipment and my home soon looked like a ghost-hunting set on TV. My dining room was now the "command center," and there were cameras placed throughout the house. Each of the team members were equipped with digital cameras, voice recorders, flashlights, K-2 meters, etc.

With a final check of the equipment and the lights turned out, Christy came into the house and asked everyone except for Cathy to wait outside while she walked through the house. Wes and I, along with the rest of the team, stepped out onto the porch. The weather hadn't improved. In addition to it being cold and foggy, it was now also drizzling. When the drizzle turned to rain, I suggested we go to the shop and wait.

With the temperatures still falling, Wes put some logs in the wood-burning stove and we all huddled around the fire. The team knew we had also reported activity in the shop, so they asked what we had experienced there.

Sitting around the fire, I began telling them about Albert. By the time Christy finished her walk-through of the house, part of the team had decided to stay and investigate the shop. Before Christy went back to the house, she told us that during her walk-through she'd encountered a young boy by the name of Timmy. Her impression was that he was probably about eight years old and had lived somewhere in the period of the 1920s to the 1940s. She thought Timmy was buried in the cemetery located close to our house.

The investigation had barely started and my mind was already reeling. *A child...* I'd hoped the team would find evidence of paranormal activity, but I wasn't prepared to hear about the ghost of a child. Being a mother, this was a place my mind didn't want to go. Even though I'd always wondered why we experienced so much activity, I had never considered the possibility that it came from the cemetery.

Christy continued telling us of her impressions. She said she thought Timmy looked to Wes and me as parental figures. She felt that he used to stay more in the children's rooms, but since they'd moved, he tended to play in the computer room because that's where I spent a lot of my time.

Christy's impressions, at least in part, were accurate. The activity in the computer room had increased once the children left home and I'd never mentioned to her or any member of the team that I worked out of the computer room, yet she somehow knew that's where I spent most of my time.

As I tried to process this information, Christy said they were ready for the next phase of the investigation.

She and half the team went back into the house while Wes, the other investigators, and I stayed in the shop.

I'm not able to see very well in the dark, so I pulled up a chair and sat quietly as they turned off the lights and started the investigation. Not being able to participate, my mind kept going back to the things Christy had said. *Had her impressions been correct? Did we have the ghost of a little boy living with us?*

Even though I didn't want to think of the ghost as being a child, I'd suspected it once before myself. Like now, it had been too hard to think about, so I chose not to. I now wondered if "Timmy" could've been the same ghost from all those years ago.

When my children were in elementary school, I'd gotten into the habit of taking a nap before it was time to pick them up. After lying down, I'd feel someone crawl over my legs and lie down beside me. A few minutes before my alarm went off, I'd wake feeling someone crawl back over me and out of the bed. If I didn't get up at that point, I'd feel a little push on my shoulder.

Jolting me back to the investigation, I heard one of the investigators exclaim, "Did you see that?"

Personally, I couldn't see much of anything, but I heard Wes say he'd seen a shadow pass in front of the window. I listened as he and the investigator talked about how the shadow had completely blocked out what little moonlight was coming in through the window.

Wes, several of our employees, and I had all seen shadows in the shop before. Typically, it was in the shape of a man and it would pass in front of the window, go down the long wall then disappear when it reached the back of the shop.

Without being able to see, I knew this must be what they were witnessing. Within a few seconds of the first investigator saying he saw the shadow, another investigator in the back of the shop claimed to see it in the beam of his flashlight.

As the shop team continued to investigate, there were no more reports of seeing anything unusual. One investigator said he felt a tug on his sleeve and we'd all heard several unexplainable noises, but we could only hope their equipment had captured something tangible to back up the claims.

The team investigating the house hoped for the same. They, too, had many personal experiences. Christy said they had started their investigation by doing a base reading of the electromagnetic field. She said that one of the investigators had taken the K-2 meter into my bedroom and set it on my bed. After a few minutes, the meter spiked. They couldn't come up with a "normal" reason as to why this would happen. She said the meter ended up spiking twice in my bedroom and once in the hall outside of my door.

As she continued to tell me about their experiences, she said that two of the investigators had seen a shadow in the hall, and around the same time they thought they heard someone say "Hey." Another investigator saw a face peer around the corner in the dining room, then again in the kitchen, and also heard the word "Hey" spoken aloud.

After sharing these experiences with us, Christy told Wes and me that she'd met another entity in what was once our daughter's room. She said she thought his name might be George. She felt he had been a farmer and was killed in some type of accident involving a horse. She said she didn't think we had anything to worry about with him. She did think he was a little grouchy and wanted to be left alone.

The word "grouchy" rang true to me. I could remember Keshia using the same word to describe one of the entities in her room. If Christy was right and he wanted to be left alone, that could also explain why her door would slam shut on the occasions I left it open.

As we talked, she said she thought "George" was also buried in the cemetery and that he might actually be Timmy's grandpa. She said the ghosts seemed to be drawn here and she asked if I'd ever helped them.

Envisioning what I'd seen on TV with ghosts getting someone to help them solve their own murder or some such thing, I told her no. I explained Keshia and I simply acknowledged them and let them know we knew they were here.

Christy explained that we made them feel safe and by acknowledging them, we had in essence put a beacon on top of our house. With us living so close to the cemetery, she said she thought we had probably experienced a lot of activity over the years.

I knew she was at least right about that.

31: IMPRESSIONS

. . . .

The investigation of our home by OKPRI was a positive experience. In the end, the tangible evidence turned out to be less than what any of us had hoped. The only substantiation of the claims that took place the night of the investigation were two separate recordings of a disembodied voice saying "Hey." Both of these recordings were audible to the investigators at the time of the investigation, so they weren't classified as an EVP. It was a good piece of evidence, but as always, I'd wanted more.

With all the personal experiences that took place that night, I'd hoped one of the shadows or faces would've been captured on someone's camera; or even better, live video footage of one of the apparitions would've been nice. After living with and investigating ghosts, I've learned that tangible evidence doesn't always come easy.

When most of us think of finding evidence of ghosts, we tend to think of capturing EVPs, pictures, or video footage. As exciting as those are, I've learned that impressions deserve consideration as well. Generally, this can only be classified as a personal experience, but there are times when these impressions come with some validation.

It wasn't unusual for Keshia and me to receive the same impressions from a ghost. The most memorable account took place a short time after Wes and I returned home from the first ghost-hunters seminar.

Wes and I decided to take advantage of the beautiful spring day and go for a walk out in the field. Reaching the wooded area of our land, we made a makeshift seat from a fallen tree. As we sat and talked, I started feeling very uncomfortable. I told Wes about these feelings and he suggested I take what we'd learned from the seminar and try to figure out what was making me feel that way.

At the seminar, we'd learned feelings like this were sometimes caused by place memories. I closed my eyes and within minutes, I had what looked like clips from a movie flashing through my mind. I could see clouds of smoke and there were people and horses running in different directions. In the middle of all this confusion, the "movie" abruptly stopped. With my eyes closed, I saw a still image of a man's boot that was stuck in the mud.

I opened my eyes and looked around. The contrast between what I saw and the "movie" that had run through my mind was vastly different. In reality, it was a gorgeous and peaceful sun-filled day. When I closed my eyes again, the movie continued. I could see charred teepees dotting the land. It reminded me of the old westerns I used to watch with my dad when I was young. Having the knowledge that Indians once occupied our land, I tried convincing myself that these scenes were merely remembrances of one of those old movies.

Still sitting with my eyes closed, I saw a "picture" of an Indian woman. Like the boot, it was a still image and it flashed on and off in my mind. Each time I saw the picture, I would feel an overwhelming sense of panic. Even though the woman never spoke, I had the most horrible feeling that the owner of the boot had raped and killed her. My chest tightened and it was hard to breathe. I got up from our seat and told Wes I was going home.

As I rushed through the field, I noticed the further we got from the tree the better I felt. Slowing my pace, I told Wes about the movie and the pictures I'd seen in my mind. Trying to convince myself as much as him, I said I was sure the images must have come from an old movie.

He told me not to discount the experience just yet because he had a confession to make. He said he had specifically taken me to that area to see if I'd pick up on anything because when he was a kid, he hated going down there. He went on to say that during the seminar, when they talked about how places sometimes retained memories, he thought of that particular place.

After we made it back to the house, Wes called out for Keshia and asked her if she had time to go for a walk with him. I knew his intentions were to see if Keshia would pick up on any of the same things I had. Being back in the safety of my home, the encounter seemed surreal. I clung to the hope that it had all been the product of an overactive imagination.

That hope ended when Wes and Keshia returned. Not knowing why Wes had taken her to the tree, she told him she felt something very bad had happened there long ago. She talked about the smoke, the chaos, and the woman. The only difference between our stories was she never mentioned the boot.

With Keshia and I both getting the same impression, I was afraid the things we saw that day may have actually happened. I could only hope they didn't. There are times impressions prove to be much more than thoughts or feelings.

This next account may seem a little evasive. I do this to prevent any unnecessary pain to the deceased family members of the person I'm referring to.

Wes and I had an acquaintance that I'll call Randy. We didn't know him very well, which is one reason this experience shook me to my very core.

I was in my living room one day looking out the window. When I turned around, I saw a vision of Randy standing in the doorway between the living room and dining room. I use the word vision only because I don't know what else to call it. This "vision" wasn't a solid form. If someone else had been standing beside me, I don't think they would have seen anything out of the ordinary. This was only in my mind, but seeing it stopped me in my tracks. The whole encounter couldn't have lasted more than a few seconds. But, as I stood speechlessly gawking at the doorway, Randy said, "I didn't know you could do this." He then went on to tell me he'd committed suicide.

As I mentioned before, I didn't know Randy very well and I couldn't imagine why I would have such a thought. As far as I knew, Randy was alive and well, but this incident weighed heavy on my mind all day. After Wes came home, I relayed the experience to him. Like me, he didn't have any idea as to why this would happen. His suggestion was that I try to forget the whole thing.

As hard as I tried to follow his advice, I couldn't. Thoughts of the vision plagued me for the rest of the evening. The next morning I vowed not to dwell on it and I started my day as usual. Wes left for work and I began doing my morning household chores. When the phone rang and I heard Wes's voice on the other end asking me if I was sitting down, I knew I wasn't going to like what he had to say.

Wes had stopped in at a local convenience store on his way to work, and was told that Randy had committed suicide the day before. The words literally brought me to my knees. I knew what Wes was saying was true. What I didn't know was why Randy had come to me and told me what he'd done.

This incident has bothered me for years, not just that it happened, which was bad enough, but all the "whys" that surrounded it. There were so many things I didn't— and to be honest, still don't—understand. But during the investigation, Christy had said that we'd unknowingly placed a beacon on our house. If that's true, I guess it's possible that like the others, Randy just saw the beacon.

32: KATE

....

Dealing with ghosts is always easier when I think of them as being people I never knew. However, not having ever known them doesn't mean the experiences can't be validated. Wes and I found this out in an unusual way while spending another weekend at the Crescent Hotel.

Sitting in a beautiful corner room surrounded by windows, we reminisced about the various times we'd visited the hotel. Some of our fondest memories were of attending the seminars. Just starting our vacation, we decided meditating would be beneficial in helping us to prepare our minds for a relaxing weekend. We each picked a chair and sat quietly as we tried to clear our minds. I hadn't meditated in awhile and I found it hard to quiet my mind. I finally gave up and sat in silence, hoping Wes was having better luck.

After twenty minutes or so, he opened his eyes and shook his head a few times. He leaned over in his chair and, now resting his elbows on his knees with his chin in his hands, he stared straight ahead. Seeing his blank gaze, I asked if he was okay.

He wagged his head from side to side, then, sitting up straight, he told me he just had the strangest dream ... or thing ... happen to him.

I waited, expecting him to say something else, but he quietly stared straight ahead. Prodding him, I finally asked him to tell me what had happened.

His eyes had a faraway look as he told me that he had just seen a woman. Shaking his head again, he corrected himself and said, "Or part of a woman." Then once again, he fell silent.

We'd meditated many times together and I'd never seen him react this way before. I didn't know what he'd seen or thought he'd seen, but he was starting to worry me a little bit. I called out his name and again asked him if he was okay.

He nodded and told me he had seen a woman's hands as she was bending over lacing up a white boot. He paused, then added that the boots were tall and had brass hooks. He shut his eyes as if he were trying to remember. He said,

"She had on a white dress, too. I could see the bottom of it as she laced up her boot. She said, 'My name's Kate, or you can call me Katherine—but not Katie.'" He went on to say he got the feeling she wasn't very happy about something.

This was a bit strange. Wes didn't usually get impressions and I wasn't picking up on anything other than the fact that we weren't alone, which wasn't an unusual feeling at the Crescent Hotel. I asked him if he was getting anything else.

He pointed and shook his finger as he asked me the name of the man who was responsible for building the hotel.

Being a frequent visitor of the Crescent, I had tried to learn a lot of its history. I'd told Wes before that a man by the name of Powell Clayton was instrumental in bringing about the construction of the Crescent Hotel. I asked him if that was who he was talking about.

He nodded as he told me he thought the woman wearing the white boot was related to him in some way. He said he thought she might have been his daughter.

Knowing some of the local history, I knew Powell Clayton had served as governor in the state of Arkansas. I also knew he was married and had several children, but I didn't know any of their names. Since he had been a prominent figure at the hotel, I thought we might be able to find more information at the front desk. I'd come to learn that much of the staff was well educated on the Crescent's history.

After talking to the concierge, we purchased a brochure that outlined the history of the hotel. We hoped to learn more about Powell Clayton and his family, but the booklet only talked of him and his endeavors associated with the hotel. Not learning anything new, I vowed to research it when I had access to the Internet.

Once we got home, I typed the words "Powell Clayton Arkansas Governor" into my search engine. I was shocked to see how much had actually been written about this man. I soon learned that being the ninth governor of Arkansas was only one of the many things he had accomplished. Before becoming the governor of Arkansas, he served as a brigadier general during the civil war. After serving as governor, he served as a senator and as an ambassador to Mexico.

There was a lot of information written about Powell Clayton but thus far, I hadn't found anything about whether or not he had a daughter by the name of Kate. I read and read and read. I learned more about Powell Clayton than I'd ever intended to learn. Then finally, I found mention of his family. I learned he had married a woman by the name of Adeline McGraw and they had two, or possibly even three, daughters and two sons—one of whom died in infancy. The names of the children were not mentioned.

Out of pure frustration, I typed in the names Kate and Katherine Clayton. Not even knowing if this person had ever existed, I halfheartedly scrolled through my choices of articles. Stumbling upon the archives of the *New York Times,* I skimmed through a newspaper clipping dated November 30, 1904. The piece said, " ... the engagement between her sister, Katherine Clayton and A.C. Grant Duff, Secretary of the British Legation in Mexico had been broken ... "

Mexico, I thought. *Wasn't that where Powell Clayton ...* I read the next line. "Miss Clayton is the daughter of General Powell Clayton, American Ambassador to Mexico."

Katherine Clayton, the daughter of Powell Clayton, was real! Wes had been right! And there was only one way he could've known—she told him.

Finding out Katherine Clayton had existed sent me back to the *New York Times* archives many times. It was there I learned that while Powell Clayton served as an Ambassador to Mexico, his daughters, Charlotte and Katherine, also referred to as Kathleen, met their future husbands.

Charlotte married Baron Mencheur, a Belgian Minister at Washington. And even though there had been a broken engagement, Katherine did eventually marry Arthur Grant Duff, a newly assigned British Minister to Cuba, who, according to the papers was "much her senior." Being from such a prominent family, Katherine's broken engagement and eventual marriage to the much-older Arthur Grant Duff was quite a scandal.

Attesting to just how influential this family was, according to an article dated Oct. 25, 1908, when Powell Clayton's daughter, Charlotte, now known as Baroness Moncheur, produced an heir, her husband received personal congratulations from President Roosevelt.

Even though I found the articles interesting, they didn't hold the answers I was looking for. I hoped to find even more to validate Wes's encounter with Katherine. Ideally, I would've liked to find an article that said something about how she didn't like to be called Katie, or better yet an article that talked about her favorite pair of white boots with brass eyes. Since that hadn't happened, I'd have to be satisfied with just knowing that Katherine Clayton did exist and that she at one time had ties to the Crescent Hotel. According to the hotel's history, the Clayton family lived at the hotel in the Governor's suite when Katherine was a child.

33: CONCLUSION

• •

There are many things about the paranormal I don't claim to understand. How or even why some of us receive impressions would be at the top of this list. Personally, I don't believe this is any special gift that has been bestowed on only a few, but a trait we all possess when we allow ourselves to be aware of our surroundings. Living with ghosts and studying the paranormal has taught me one thing and that is never to doubt the uncertainty of this world.

Coming out of my shell and learning to talk about my experiences helped me see that many people believe in ghosts. What surprises me is the level of fear associated with that belief. I recently started a blog where I encourage people to talk about their own personal experiences with the paranormal.

Through this blog, I've found that the people who have had experiences of their own tend to be much less frightened than the ones who haven't. Typically, they don't want to post their experiences publicly, but choose to send me a private message, which usually reads much like my own encounters with reports of non-violent, subtle activity.

Those who haven't had an experience are usually terrified at the prospect. Things we don't understand often generate fear. I hope this book will give some insight to those seeking answers and perhaps comfort those who are afraid.

I am not asking anyone to open their minds so wide that their brains fall out. But we should all acknowledge that there is so much about our world that we may never fully understand. The best that we can do is to listen to the perspectives of others and make our own decisions. To that end, I've asked Keshia to share her unique perspective on growing up with ghosts.

Epilogue:
The Next Generation
by Keshia Swaim

As a child, ghosts taught me that thunderstorms were nothing to be afraid of, tucked me in at night, and were very good at playing hide-and-seek. I didn't—and still don't—know how or why they exist, but I didn't know how or why birds fly either. But people never question the fact that birds do indeed fly. To me, ghosts fell into the same category. I don't remember when I decided that the green ball in my room was a ghost, but I don't think it was ever a big deal. Ghosts were just part of life; nothing to get too excited about. It wasn't until much later that I discovered not everyone felt that way.

Of course, I knew that some people were afraid of ghosts. My friend Cindy, along with various cartoons and horror shows, taught me that ghosts made a lot of people scared. But so do spiders, and I had a pet tarantula. I think my earliest knowledge that ghosts were not something everyone saw came from my dad. Imagine my surprise when I first heard him deny the existence of something I saw on a daily basis! In my mind, the only way to explain his skepticism was to decide that dear old Dad just wasn't all there. His staunch refusal to acknowledge the spirits in our home, even when they did exactly what he told them to do, became a standing joke between Mom and me. To my shock, over the years, I realized that Dad was the normal one.

Most people didn't believe in ghosts. And even among the believers, ghosts were not something people typically wanted around. I do understand that some people have had frightening experiences that they attribute to ghosts. Some of my own encounters have been unpleasant, and a few were truly frightening. But I can say the same thing about my experiences with people. If I decided that I no longer wanted people around me, or chose to ignore their existence, I'd be nuts. So why would I shun ghosts as a whole because of a few bad apples? Besides, I have a feeling that ghosts are a lot like us. Some of them are mean, but very few are really evil. And, like people, most of the ones that initially seem mean are not so bad if we take the time to get to know them.

Needless to say, discovering I was in the minority as a ghost-lover did not dissuade me from talking about them. Instead, I became more interested in the paranormal: watching TV specials, reading about ghosts, going on ghost tours, and being very open about my beliefs and experiences.

My first "real job" gave me plenty to talk about. I worked at a local pizzeria through high school, and I quickly discovered that the employees were not the only ones in the kitchen. Before I go any further, let me set the stage by stating that I'm fairly short; five feet with my shoes on. While preparing pizzas to go in the oven, I constantly had to ask my taller co-workers to hand me cooking utensils that I had just placed on the edge of the buffet, only to find that they had slid to the back, well out of my reach. After several co-workers jokingly told me to stop throwing things where I couldn't reach them, I calmly explained that I was being picked on by the resident ghost. They all shook their heads and looked at me like I was crazy. Even when we occasionally got stuck in the walk-in freezer, as if someone was holding the door shut, and the chime above the entry door sounded for no apparent reason, I was the crazy one who believed in ghosts.

I can only recall one instance that made one of them take me seriously. A female co-worker and I were standing in a storage room talking when we should have been working. Our conversation was interrupted when a two-gallon glass jar, half-full of peppers, slid off a shelf and fell about six feet to the concrete floor. The crash got our attention, but to our complete surprise, the jar didn't break. Instead, it bounced a few times, like a basketball, before coming to a stop, upright, in front of us. Without thinking about it, I griped at the ghost: "Geez, you don't have to give us heart attacks. We're going."

It wasn't until I'd given up on lifting the heavy jar above my head to put it back on the shelf that I noticed my co-worker was much paler than usual. The ghost's stunt had startled me, too, but nothing was broken, so, the way I saw it, no harm done. And he (it was definitely male) was right; we both had jobs we should have been doing instead of talking about boys. So I was genuinely at a loss.

"Hey, are you okay?" I asked, choosing a spot for the peppers on a rack much closer to the ground. "You don't look so good. Are you sick?"

She shook her head. "You really believe in this ghost stuff, huh?"

"Well, yeah." I was finally catching on. "But it's not usually like the stuff on TV. I've never actually been hurt by one, they're pretty harmless, I think. They just want attention."

"But you really think there is a ghost here? Like, a dead person is messing with us?"

I could tell she halfway believed me, and if I wasn't careful, she was going to have a panic attack, right here between the flour and spices. "I honestly don't know if ghosts are dead people. But whatever it is, I think of it as more cool than scary."

"Cool?" She raised a very skeptical eyebrow.

"Well, think about it. Neither one of us touched that shelf. And even if we did, it would have taken a pretty hard jolt to knock a heavy jar of peppers to the ground. But the cool part is that it didn't break." I could tell she didn't see why that was cool, but the color was coming back to her cheeks, so I continued. "How could glass fall that far, hit concrete, and not even crack? You've gotta admit, it's at least interesting."

She just shook her head again. "You're sure it isn't going to hurt me or follow me home or anything?"

I just shrugged. I couldn't tell her that ghosts, like people, weren't 100 percent predictable, so instead I laughed. "It hasn't happened yet, has it?"

My answer seemed good enough for her, and we'd already spent too much time not making pizzas, so the subject was dropped and we went back to work. Later, the guy responsible for taking inventory demanded to know who put the peppers in the wrong spot. Between the "don't you dare" glare I was getting from my friend, and the customers that could hear the conversation, I knew this was not the time or place for another ghost conversation. So I just gave him my sweetest smile and answered, "Some of us aren't big and strong enough to put them back on the top shelf." My friend relaxed, my customers laughed, and the shift manager's ears turned red. I had mastered the art of dealing with spooky situations without lying or freaking anyone out.

It was a skill I had to use a lot. Over the years, I discovered that my high school, college, every place I have lived, every place I have worked, and several of my favorite vacation spots have ghosts attached to them. And since half my family, most of my friends, and the vast majority of my co-workers are extremely uncomfortable with the idea that they share their space with beings they can't see, I've learned to pretend I don't notice a lot.

Ghosts are honestly not something I think about every day. They are always around, and ghostly activity is so commonplace that turning on a light isn't going to get my attention. It usually takes bumping into a new entity, or an old one doing something drastic, like throwing model cars at me, to make me pause and think about how abnormal my life really is. One afternoon, while regaling my husband, Stephen, with stories of my haunted childhood, a truly creepy thought struck me: Do ghosts follow me? Which is more likely; every place I've spent much time at is haunted, or I am simply a haunted person?

I've heard the theory before that ghosts can sense "sensitive" people, and they are drawn to them. To get a better picture of this idea, I'll reference *Ghost Town*. It is a quirky film in which the main character has a near-death experience that lets him see ghosts. One ghost discovers the poor man's new ability and tells another, until every ghost in the city has taken up residence in his apartment. Although the film is a comedy, the thought that it might be accurate in its portrayal of sensitives gives me goose bumps. I do not like the idea that I could make a place haunted, simply by being there.

So, perhaps selfishly, I have decided that this theory is wrong. There are ghosts in most places, but most people don't pay enough attention to notice them. While I do not believe that I make places haunted by spending time there, I do think that many ghosts are more active when I am around, because I give them what they want: attention. I'll use my current job to illustrate my theory.

I have worked at the same bank my entire adult career. Within a few days of starting my new position, I knew that the bank was haunted. At first, there were no major incidents, just a feeling of being watched. That is creepy enough, especially working after-hours in a bank, when I was certain I was alone. But, the longer I worked there, the more I realized that I had a rather active ghost on my hands. The 10-key calculators at the teller stations would frequently begin typing by themselves—while they were turned off. I overheard our security officer complain that the motion sensors constantly went off, even when the security cameras clearly showed that no one was in the area. On one occasion, this happened at four a.m. and the police were dispatched to surround a completely empty building.

For months I said nothing. I simply shook my head and smiled at the reasons my co-workers came up with to explain the strange happenings in our office. Apparently, as a young professional, it is not acceptable to believe in ghosts. But it is perfectly acceptable to blame "extremely glitchy equipment" and "office gremlins" for everything that goes wrong. For example, it was not at all uncommon for faxes to arrive with missing or blank pages. Two fax machines and countless repairmen later, the "glitch" remains.

I finally decided to break my silence after I saw our resident ghost. Working on my computer one afternoon, I happened to glance at my security camera and noticed that a customer was standing in the lobby behind me, not being served. I quickly spun my chair around and stood to greet ... an empty lobby. I walked around my desk and looked for the mysterious customer. Both entrances were vacant, and none of the other employees seemed to have noticed the strange man. And this was a man they would have noticed. He was an elderly man wearing overalls and a wide-brimmed straw hat. My immediate assumption was that he was a farmer, which, given our rural location, would not have been unusual.

What was unusual was the man's height. As I walked back to my desk, I eyed the column the vanishing customer was standing near. For his hat to have reached the design on the column, which I was certain it had, the man would have to have been nearly seven feet tall. I was sure that someone would have noticed a giant, elderly farmer running through the bank. But no one else had seen a thing.

From that point on, I started talking to our ghost and blaming him for our numerous "glitches." I believe that by doing so, I painted a huge target on myself. Most of my co-workers, of course, thought I was nuts. And the few who believed I might be on to something looked at me like I'd grown another head when I told them that, yes, I liked ghosts; in fact, they had been friends of mine for years.

But the target I spoke of was for the ghost. Almost as soon as I started acknowledging him, things started vanishing from my desk. I was frequently touched, heard my name called, and saw flashes of movement when nobody else was in the area. Usually, I didn't mind this type of attention. It was almost like a game to me, and it kept work a little more interesting.

That is, until the day he crossed the line. Late one afternoon, as I was getting things in order so that I could leave, I experienced one of a banker's worst fears. I was missing a check. A very large one. I distinctly remembered it because it was lime green, and worth about half my annual salary. I knew I had placed it in a black plastic tray on my desk, but it simply wasn't there. After frantically searching, I called in two of my co-workers to help me find the check. We dug through trash bins, emptied desk drawers, crawled under desks, and anything else we could think of.

After approximately half an hour, I was about to have a panic attack. And then one of the women found the check. Lime green, face-up, in the black tray I had placed it in earlier. I stomped my foot, told the ghost he had gone too far and to never touch my work again, and then I went home. After I left, the other two women decided that, in our desperate search, one of us had accidentally picked up the check and, not realizing what she had, placed it exactly where it was supposed to go.

I decided not to argue the point. I knew what had happened, and more importantly, the ghost knew I would only put up with him to a certain point. He's never messed with my work again. That is not to say he's left me alone. His new trick is locking me out of certain areas of the bank. We have electronic finger scans that allow access to parts of our branch. The scans work for all of the employees, except me, unless I beg, or insult the door. For instance, if I say, "Let me in, you stupid piece of crap" before scanning my finger, I will normally be able to open the door. I know it's possible that I trigger some kind of malfunction with the door, but I think the more likely explanation is that the ghost wants me to know he's still around.

But my current ghostly experiences are not limited to work. As Mom mentioned, my house is haunted. The ghosts at my new home are not nearly as active as the ones where I grew up. And, to be honest, I'm a bit disappointed. I think at least one of these ghosts and I got off on the wrong foot. He was not happy when we moved in, and his intimidation tactics just annoyed me. After a year of trying to upset Stephen and me, I think he just got bored. He's still around. I can feel him from time to time, hovering in a corner, or out back under a shade tree.

There is at least one other ghost that shares our home, but she is very shy. I can't list a single thing that she has done. I simply know she's there. Sometimes I wish I had more time to spend at home. Maybe then I'd be able to draw her out of her shell a little bit. I keep hoping that eventually "my ghosts" will warm up to me, and I can continue to have the types of experiences I had as a child.

But, recently, I think our ghosts have found something else to occupy their attention. Since moving into our home, Stephen and I have been blessed with a son. He isn't old enough to speak yet, but frequently he stares down an empty hall, or doorway. His eyes move as if he is watching something, and occasionally he'll laugh out loud, and I can't help but wonder what he sees. Whatever it is, he doesn't seem at all afraid.

GHOST
UNDER FOOT
The Spirit of Mary Bell

A TRUE STORY OF ONE FAMILY'S HAUNTING

KENNETH W. HARMON

A Haunted Love Story
The Ghosts of the Allen House
MARK SPENCER

A Haunted Love Story is two tales in one: a modern family's attempt to embrace their strange, spirit-inhabited home and a vintage love affair kept secret for six decades.

When Mark Spencer bought the beautiful old Allen House in Monticello, Arkansas, he knew that it was famously haunted. According to ghost lore, the troubled spirit of Ladell Allen, who mysteriously commited suicide in the master bedroom in 1948, still roamed the historic mansion. Yet Mark remained skeptical—until he and his family began witnessing faceless phantoms, a doppelganger spirit, and other paranormal phenomena. Ensuing ghost investigations offered convincing evidence that six spirits, including Ladell, inhabited their home. But the most shocking event occured the day Spencer followed a strange urge to explore the attic and found, crammed under a floorboard, secret love letters that touchingly depict Ladell Allen's forbidden, heart-searing romance—and shed light on her tragic end.

978-0-7387-3073-8, 240 pp., 5³⁄₁₆ x 8   **$15.95**

Marcus F. Griffin
Foreword by Jeff Belanger

EXTREME
PARANORMAL
INVESTIGATIONS

The Blood Farm Horror,
the Legend of Primrose Road,
and Other Disturbing Hauntings

Extreme Paranormal Investigations
The Blood Farm Horror, the Legend of Primrose Road, and Other Disturbing Hauntings
Marcus F. Griffin

Set foot inside the bone-chilling, dangerous, and sometimes downright terrifying world of extreme paranormal investigations. Join Marcus F. Griffin, a Wiccan priest and founder of Witches in Search of the Paranormal (WISP), as he and his team explore the Midwest's most haunted properties. These investigations include the creepiest-of-the-creepy cases WISP has tackled over the years, many of them in locations that had never before been investigated. These true-case files include investigations of Okie Pinokie and the Demon Pillar Pigs, the Ghost Children of Munchkinland Cemetery, and the Legend of Primrose Road. Readers will also get an inside glimpse of previously inaccessible places, such as the former Jeffrey Dahmer property as WISP searches for the notorious serial killer's spirit, and the farm that belonged to Belle Gunness, America's first female serial killer and the perpetrator of the Blood Farm Horror.

978-0-7387-2697-7, 264 pp., 5³⁄₁₆ x 8   **$15.95**

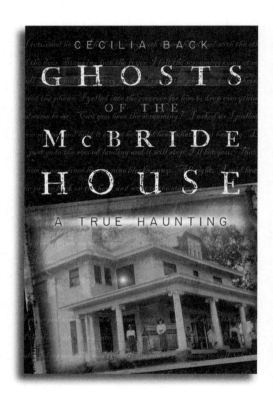

CECILIA BACK

GHOSTS

OF THE

McBRIDE

HOUSE

A TRUE HAUNTING

Ghosts of the McBride House
A True Haunting
Cecilia Back

It took Cecilia Back only a few weeks to confirm that her new home—a Victorian mansion just across the street from a historic military fort—was haunted. But instead of fleeing, the Back family stayed put and gradually got to know their "spirited" residents over the next twenty-five years.

Meet Dr. McBride, the original owner who loves scaring away construction crews and the author's ghost-phobic mother. Try to catch sight of the two spirit children who play with Back's son and daughter and loud, electronic toys in the middle of the night. Each ghost has a personality of its own, including one transient entity whose antics are downright terrifying.

Despite mischievous pranks, such as raucous ghost parties at two a.m., the Back family have come to accept—and occasionally welcome—these unique encounters with the dead.

978-0-7387-1505-6, 216 pp., 5³⁄₁₆ x 8   **$14.95**

PARANORMAL OBSESSION

OBSESSION

America's Fascination with
Ghosts & Hauntings, Spooks & Spirits

DEONNA KELLI SAYED

Paranormal Obsession
America's Fascination with Ghosts & Hauntings, Spooks & Spirits
Deonna Kelli Sayed

Why is America so captivated by the unexplained? Far beyond a book of ghost stories, *Paranormal Obsession* offers a unique cultural studies approach to the global phenomena of spirits, ghost hunting, and all things otherworldly.

Providing an insider's view from within the spirit-seeking community, paranormal investigator Deonna Kelli Sayed explores how and why our love of spirits started, how ghosts took over the small screen, the roles of science and religion, our fascination with life after death—and what it all says about American culture.

Weighing perspectives of ghost hunters, religious figures, scientists, academics, parapsychologists, and cast members of the popular TV shows *Ghost Hunters* and *Paranormal State*, this book offers compelling insight into Americans' fixation on ghostly activity. It also highlights the author's paranormal group's investigation of the *USS North Carolina*, the most haunted battleship in the United States.

978-0-7387-2635-9, 264 pp., 6 x 9   **$15.95**

TRUE POLICE STORIES

OF THE
STRANGE & UNEXPLAINED

Detective Sergeant Ingrid P. Dean
FOREWORD BY Kathryn Harwig

True Police Stories of
the Strange & Unexplained
Ingrid P. Dean

Divine protection from angels, bizarre synchronistic events, stunning miracles that defy logic. Police officers experience the strange and extraordinary all the time, but rarely talk about it. *True Police Stories of the Strange & Unexplained* offers a rare and gripping glimpse inside their perilous day-to-day lives.

These true, first-hand accounts from law enforcement officials across the nation reveal how intuition, apparitions, UFOs, prophetic dreams, and other forces beyond our understanding have impacted them in the course of duty. From death-defying gun battles to thrilling rescues to heart-searing tragedies, and even a few comical encounters, these truly amazing tales shed light on what our police force faces every day—and expose the fascinating inner lives of the heroic men and women behind the badge.

978-0-7387-2644-1, 288 pp., 5³⁄₁₆ x 8   **$15.95**